"As a student of many books in this genre, this is the first I've read that gave a clear, concise description of the ego/soul relationship in an understandable way. Accented by Aila's personal journey, her struggles and techniques for success makes this book relatable to all who read it. I was riveted and finished the *The Call Of The Soul* feeling clearer, more hopeful, energized to change the patterns in my life which have kept me stuck. Closing the last chapter opened a new chapter in my life."

—Robert Cuccioli, Tony-nominated Broadway actor
and singer

"Having known the life crisis that sends the head spinning, the body stalling, and leaves the soul smothered, Aila Accad has stepped into the light of change! In this, her latest volume, *The Call Of The Soul*, she takes us through the methodology of listening and responding to the soul's whispering call, until eventually we are hearing it loud and clear! Aila is a regular radio guest of mine. The listener response has been strong and positive regarding her weekly Stress Busting tips! If you're looking for the ultimate self-help book, may I suggest a thorough introduction to your soul and the help of Aila Accad!"

—Ric Cochran, poet and radio host, West Virginia
Radio Corp

D0370234

THE CALL
OF THE SOUL

A PATH TO KNOWING YOUR TRUE
SELF AND YOUR LIFE'S PURPOSE

By

AILA ACCAD,
RN, MSN

A division of
The Career Press, Inc.
Pompton Plains, NJ

THE CALL OF THE SOUL
EDITED BY JODI BRANDON
TYPESET BY EILEEN MUNSON
Cover design by Joanna Williams
Printed in the U.S.A.

To order this title, please call toll-free 1-800-CAREER-1 (NJ and Canada: 201-848-0310) to order using VISA or MasterCard, or for further information on books from Career Press.

The Career Press, Inc.
220 West Parkway, Unit 12
Pompton Plains, NJ 07444
www.careerpress.com
www.newpagebooks.com

Library of Congress Cataloging-in-Publication Data
Accad, Aila.
    The call of the soul : a path to knowing your true self and your life's purpose / by Aila Accad, RN, MSN.
        pages cm
    Includes index.
    ISBN 978-1-60163-274-6 -- ISBN 978-1-60163-519-8 (ebook)
    1. Self-realization. 2. Self-acceptance. 3. Self-acceptance-- Religious aspects. I. Title.

BF637.S4A34 2013
158.1--dc23
                                                    2013012534

Dedicated to my sister
Patty.

You are forever in my heart.

⁂

Acknowledgments

Words fall short to express the deep gratitude I feel for all the people and experiences that brought me to this moment.

To my wonderful family, whose souls grace my life in so many ways, especially grandparents; parents; sisters, Patrice and Joan, and brother, Bob; children, Aaron, Beth, and Jerry; and precious grandchildren, Martina, Eden, Aillea, and Alfred, who delightfully connect me with the child's soul.

All my amazing teachers and guides, especially JR Keener, Rennie Moran, Linda Krier, John Davis, and my dear fellow travelers in Diamond Heart III.

My brave and brilliant clients, who chose transformation and afforded me the privilege to travel with them as their guide; you always inspire my soul.

My cherished friends, whose support and feedback are priceless, especially Barbie Dallman, who coached me to trust my knowing, and Joyce Almond, who called then, coaxed me to meet my immensely supportive literary agent, Lisa Hagan. Her words *"I want that book. Send me a proposal!"* still make my heart leap.

The soulful Diamond Women, Paula Bickham, Rita Ray and Una Karner, who prompted me to a deeper understanding of my lessons by asking me to share the process with them each month.

The supportive friends who took precious time to share their insights at the discussion gatherings.

Most deeply to the Soul that continuously unfolds a call to grow and the Ego that lovingly adjusts to serve the soul's purpose.

And, the Consciousness that connects All.

I feel immensely blessed!

Contents

Part III
Stepping Into the Call

Preface

A bright 9-year-old girl sat on the edge of her bed in despair. She pondered what point there is in a life that is so difficult and unhappy. The firstborn of four children, she had taken on the task of making her parents happy. Because they were not happy, especially her mother, she felt like a failure. In utter frustration and desperation, her soul appealed to the only source she knew had the power to help: *"Holy Spirit, either tell me why I'm here and what this is all about, or take me back!"*

This was the beginning of my spiritual journey, my life quest. After making that demand of the Holy Spirit, a deep sense of calm instantly filled every cell of my body. In that moment, I knew that if I just keep going, one day my quest would be answered.

The journey has been amazing so far. I've engaged in many deep inner processes that ultimately brought me to a place where I feel free—a place where it is effortless to be authentic, at peace, and consistently filled with love, gratitude, and joy. In hindsight, I realize that my quest was not only to arrive at this place of expansive living. It was also to experience and understand the process of how to get here in order to share that with others.

Although there is always more to learn, my intention in writing this book at this time is to share a path I've discovered to achieve self-love, a path that is highly desired and mysteriously elusive to most of us.

I began the journey by reading everything I could get my hands on about how life works. As a result, I have a huge nonfiction library of philosophy, psychology, religion, spirituality, and self-help books, along with volumes of workshop notes. I've learned from many notable luminaries, whom I quote regularly in presentations. I met many wise teachers at Omega Institute, Common Boundary, Peak Potentials, Institute for Noetic Science, Conferences on Science and Consciousness, and more.

I've learned and practiced several forms of meditation, and experienced vision quests, shamanic soul retrieval, sweat lodges, silent retreats, walking on hot coals, and rebirthing through Holotropic Breathwork in the desert with Dr. Stan Grof. I also invested 12 years with an excellent psychotherapist and another 12 years studying the *Diamond Heart Approach* by Almass through the Ridhwan School.

Along the way, I acquired bachelor and master's nursing degrees and life coach certification; became a Reiki Master, practitioner and trainer for Emotional Freedom Techniques (EFT), Master Alignment, Heart Essence, Healing Touch; and more.

On the interpersonal journey I had a 25-year marriage; underwent infertility struggles; grieved the loss of parents, grandparents, a beloved sister, and a best friend; adopted children; lived in four states; created businesses and partnerships; mediated a marital divorce and business partnership dissolution; had a hip replacement; and lost 100 pounds three times (at last permanently).

It is my lifelong pattern to learn through experience, then turn around and teach others the essence of what I just learned. I have come to know this process as the call of my soul. That "call" consciously began at age 9 and continues today.

Prior contributions along the way include *34 Instant Stress-Busters: Quick Tips to De-Stress Fast with No Extra Time or Money, Breaking the Perfection Myth: A Model for Personal Freedom and Self-Esteem, Weight No More: A Program for Permanent Weight Release*, and *The Well: A Model for Recovery from Addiction, Depression and Spiritual Crisis.* Each of these represents a crystallization of knowledge at particular points in the journey.

I'm eager to offer this new way to conceptualize the inner relationship because the quality of the relationship with one's self is the foundation for all life experiences. Self-love, in particular, is the foundation for the most desirable and expansive life experiences: passion, purpose, love, security, joy, happiness, fulfillment, and peace, which so many are seeking at this time.

Visioning great rewards for you as you learn to hear and live the call of *your* soul!

Introduction

This book is for anyone on the quest to become whole by discovering the answers to the questions *Who am I?* and *What is my purpose?* What has called you to read it at this time in your life?

Are you wondering about your purpose? Are you curious to know more about the truth of who you are? Are you seeking a way to calm inner conflict? Are you feeling both desire and resistance to making changes in your life? You can be assured that if your soul is calling you to answer these questions and others, you will find what you are seeking!

The Quest for Your Truth

We tend to live as if our primary relationship in life is between the body we inhabit and the world in which we live. Most people believe that the outside circumstances of life determine the state of mind, body, and emotions that I call "me." We don't know, unless we are prompted by some inner or outer catalyst, that there is a more central and core relationship that holds the key to treasures we seek in the outer world. You chose to explore *that* relationship by picking this book to read.

When you understand the dynamic inner relationships that drive how you see yourself and relate with the world, the inner workings of the person you call "me," you will have the means to know your true self and transform your life. This book introduces you to your inner players and their relationships, how inner change really works, and the resources to take action.

You may have read or learned much about yourself already, yet here you are again. That happened to me, too. Kind of frustrating, isn't it? I think this happens because most of what is available is from a theoretical, esoteric, or spiritual perspective. Here is how I know that. Before sitting down to write this book, I went to Amazon and purchased every notable book I could find with *ego* or *soul* in the title, and that is what I found. While those perspectives are interesting, they are not enough.

My clients are also people who have done a lot of inner work on themselves; many are counselors and therapists. They come to me because they are still seeking some way to control an aspect of life that continues to be a source of suffering, despite all the knowledge and understanding they acquired.

Through our work together, they not only get relief, but they are ultimately empowered and confident to make new choices and construct a life grounded with more joy, love, peace, and success by their own definition.

Grounded is the operative word here. This book, though quite logical and rational, is not designed to speak exclusively to your mind. It is written to also speak to your soul, which is grounded in the experiences of your body. My intention is to describe the lived experience of your inner world with clear examples so, when you are done, you will know yourself in a real and intimate way. This is what you need in order to have the power to change your life and your experience in the world to your own satisfaction.

Hello, Your Soul Is Calling

For many of us, the quest for identity and life direction is first deeply pondered in adolescence. The "soul" of a teen or young adult bursting with creative desire attempts to break free from parental and societal "ego" structures, which feel confining. If the answers to the questions are not clear or the soul's determination not strong enough, the young person resigns to conforming to established social norms and conditioned cultural and family expectations, or rebels against them.

The ego takes charge: *Go to college, get a good job, get married, have kids, and so on* or *No way am I doing that.* When this happens, the soul's quest to be free goes underground, often to reemerge in midlife. At midlife, the conflict between the long-entrenched ego and the freedom-starved soul often manifests as a midlife crisis. For this reason, the knowledge in this book can be particularly helpful to 20-something Millennials as well as Baby Boomers.

Inner Conflict Resolved

Though freeing the soul is generally accepted as desirable on the path to self-awareness and personal freedom, self-development authors differ on what to do about the key barrier to this process: the ego. Popular approaches suggest that the ego must be suppressed, overpowered by force, transcended through meditation or adherence to spiritual laws as the Law of Attraction, or just accepted and put in service toward worldly success. *The Call of the Soul* proposes another approach.

Based on my personal experiences and results of clients in my professional coaching practice, I discovered that the inner relationship between the ego and the soul is a love story. Like any love story, this one also reflects trials, tribulations, and triumphs.

What makes this book unique is that it proposes a resolution to the inner conflict between the ego and the soul by learning to build a harmonious relationship between them through understanding, honoring, and valuing both. This creates an inner partnership based on mutual love and support rather than seeing them as embattled enemies, even though at points in the relationship this is how it can feel.

Battling or resisting any part of you blocks self-love and inner peace. There is a solution. I've discovered that you can facilitate transformation of the ego-soul relationship through awareness, compassion, and applying skillful techniques. This is what I am about to share with you.

Part I of the book raises awareness about the unique features and roles of each of the aspects of the inner relationship. In Part II, I share a step-by-step process for how to respectfully negotiate and transform the relationship between the ego and the soul, so their inner partnership can be functional, harmonious, and supportive of a soulful life in the world. Finally, Part III provides insight into techniques and teachers, and how and why these are helpful to the process of change.

It is only by participating in practices that provided real experiences of the truth of my soul and self that I can trust what I am about to share with you in this book. Everything you read here is grounded in observable experiences from me, clients, and friends. Although the names are changed in the case of clients and friends, the reported experiences are entirely accurate.

There is nothing theoretical, mystical, esoteric, or religious in these pages, nor is this book intended to challenge your current spiritual beliefs. Because the content is based in observable experience, I feel confident that you will be able to connect this information to your current spiritual or religious values. My clients and friends are an eclectic group of people with a variety of belief systems and backgrounds, including Jewish, Catholic, Protestant, Christian, Buddhist, Muslim, Unitarian, Unity, Pagan, spiritual not religious, and atheist. All have contributed to and found value in these pages.

That said, my advice to you is this: Sift the content in these pages through your own experience and see what resonates with you. Keep what is useful to you and let go of what is not useful.

In summary, *The Call of the Soul* is intended as my contribution toward easing human struggle on the path to self-knowledge, self-love, and life purpose. I found what I was seeking and discovered in the process that self-love is at the heart of everything we seek, love, joy, happiness, security, success, harmonious relationships, and more. I have full confidence that you, too, will find what you seek through hearing and living the call of your soul!

Part I
Knowing Your True Self

No one remains quite what he was when he recognizes himself.

—Thomas Mann

I awoke at 5:15 this morning with thoughts for writing this introduction to Part I of this book. There was also resistance to getting up and writing it. This is a mild, yet clear, example of the interplay between the soul calling and the ego resisting. From experience, I know that heeding the call of the soul will result in a better outcome than sleeping another hour, so I bid you good morning.

This part of the book introduces you to inner aspects of yourself that work together to inform and evolve the path of your life. They will feel familiar to you, though you may not currently think of them as four different characters playing different roles. In this section, you will learn how to recognize these characters.

Because in your eagerness to know what to *do,* you may be tempted to jump ahead to the "how to" in Part II and Part III (ask me how I know this), I strongly encourage you to read Part I. I promise it is not a perspective you have seen before. It's important to take the time to do this, because in Part II we will talk more about the interplay between these aspects of self and the process for consciously transforming their roles. Knowing the nature of these players increases your ability to be more conscious and have more control in the change process.

The primary partners in the dance of your life are the ego and the soul. Your personal ego and soul have a unique and intimate relationship, which transforms and evolves throughout life. There are two additional aspects that play a vital role in how painful or relaxed that process of living is for you; they are the enforcer and the observer.

My intention in this section is to help you understand, appreciate, and compassionately embrace *all* the inner dynamics of your life. We are amazing beings! It is remarkable how all these aspects lovingly work together to serve us.

However, just like family members, the interplay of these aspects may not feel loving sometimes. Once you understand how they each intend to serve you, it's possible to feel good about yourself even as you experience inner conflict. And, it is possible to accept yourself without judgment as you choose to radically change your life choices.

When you are conscious of the nature and role of each aspect of your inner world, you can learn to work with them and transform them. Stress is reduced and confidence increased. This allows you to become attuned to the call of your soul and feel empowered to make new choices in your life.

If you are reading this book, you have whatever you need to succeed in the process of transforming your life. Your soul called, you heard that call, and you chose, consciously or unconsciously, to live the call of your soul. Bravo!

Chapter 1

A Partnership Is Born

The passions act as winds to propel our vessel,
our reason is the pilot that steers her;
without the winds, she would not move,
without the pilot, she would be lost.

—Old French Saying

The ego and the soul are intimate and inseparable partners. The ego would not exist without the embodied soul. And the soul, which is not bound by time and space, could not experience a structured life in the body without the ego. They are partners in our dance with life.

According to A. H. Almass, founder of the *Diamond Heart Approach*, the soul has certain innate and essential qualities as curiosity, love, joy, intelligence, compassion, and strength, for example, as well as personal qualities that are unique features of your particular soul. As a participant in the Ridhwan School, founded by Almass, I experienced these qualities directly. It was this direct experience, along with my experiences in therapy and other transformative processes that form the foundation for the concepts in this book.

The ego evolves from the newly embodied soul's experiences in utero, through the birth process, and throughout life. It emerges as the soul rubs up against experience. In this way, the ego is co-created as the soul experiences life. To hate or reject the ego is to reject a part of you. Pushing against the ego creates an inner conflict that deteriorates self-esteem.

Early ego development is based on the senses. It is formed during the precognitive and preverbal stage of human development by what you hear, see, feel, smell, taste, and touch. All of the sensory data you encounter in each moment is cataloged by the mind. This information is what triggers our patterns of thinking and behaving throughout life.

I have an image of a little librarian in my head that catalogues all this data. Whenever an experience occurs that has the same image, sound, smell, or feeling as a past experience, she runs to the file cabinets and instantly pulls out memories of all the past events that relate to this current moment.

A powerful example comes to mind. I remember the first day our realtor took us to look at houses when we moved to West Virginia. She took us to a wonderful Italian restaurant in the heart of town. The minute

I walked through the front door and breathed in the fragrance, memories immediately flooded into my mind from Grandma Rose's kitchen and Sunday family dinners at her home in Brooklyn, New York, where I lived the first three years of my life. My heart opened wide, and I instantly fell in love with Charleston.

Five couples from Delaware moved to West Virginia at the same time we did in 1984. At the end of a year, we were the only ones still here. We continue to live here and, even though the restaurant is long gone, I still love this place!

Creation Stage of the Relationship

> *There is no reality except the one contained within us.*
>
> —Hermann Hesse

The ego structure evolves from the young, naïve soul's sensory perception in the absence of reason, logic, or conscious choice. In this way, the ego reflects the soul's consciousness at a kinesthetic (physical) level. We might think of this stage as the creation stage of the relationship between the ego and the soul.

Curiosity and non-judgment are present at this stage of development. The soul and the ego interplay to form impressions about life. These impressions eventually form the foundation of the ego structure. Once formed, at about age 5 or so, that structure becomes the lens through which we interpret our life experiences.

According to pain expert Dr. Norm Shealy, a newborn has only two basic fears: the fear of loud noise and the fear of falling. All other fears come from learning in the early stages of ego development. Because the ego forms from the body's sensory experience, it is tied to basic physical instincts, the primal drives of the body for pain avoidance and pleasure.

I just attended a perinatal conference where research was presented on the importance of not cutting the umbilical cord too soon and laying the baby on the mother's chest immediately at birth. The baby roots and feeds instinctively when this is done. When the baby is separated from the mother and put in a warming bassinet, even for five minutes before coming to the mother, the baby does not do this, because just that five-minute delay causes stress. This is impressive validation of how the infant responds and changes behavior based upon everything he or she experiences.

The Role of the Ego

Nothing in nature is isolated. Nothing is without reference to something else. Nothing achieves meaning apart from that which neighbors it.

—Goethe

Because it is tied to survival, one of the primary roles the ego adopts is that of protector. Its intention is to help the embodied soul stay safe and alive. The strategies the ego devises to protect the embodied soul are called defense mechanisms. These become the *modus operandi* of the ego and show up as consistent patterns of behavior in response to perceived threats over time. Keep in mind that because these patterns were developed based on subtle sensory data, they are not necessarily logical or rational on the surface or from an adult perspective.

Here is a memory that came to me many years ago in therapy that illustrates the powerful effect a simple experience of childhood can have on the ego belief system. At about a year and a half old, I was playing with building blocks with my father. He was building the blocks up and I was knocking them down, giggling, and having a great time. At one point, I was laughing deliriously as my mother came into the room. Rather annoyed, she announced, "She should be taking a nap!" My father picked me up and put me in the crib, she walked out, he walked out, and the door closed. I cried and cried, finally crying myself to sleep.

Now, this scenario would not normally be considered abusive or traumatic from an adult perspective. Yet, it had a profound effect on how I lived my life. I was very careful to hold back my natural enthusiasm and joy, out of fear of being abandoned and alone. The thought went like this: *If people really know how strongly you feel, they will leave you.* I learned to put great stock in my logic and reason, and very little if any time or energy into spontaneous play. When I had feelings of excitement, I held them back.

As the protector of the sensitive young soul, the ego develops beliefs that become behavior patterns intended to support our basic human needs on a physical, emotional, and psychological level. These patterns address needs for food, shelter, and security, as well as affection, approval, and acceptance. The ego does not come up with these ideas and behaviors in isolation from the soul, but *in relation with* our soul's own unique essence. In this way, the ego-derived false self, or "mask" that we wear, also reflects qualities of the true self.

In the example I just shared about the pattern I call *"Don't get too excited. Everyone will leave you!"* the solution my ego evolved not only protected me from abandonment, but it also intended to preserve my soul's deep yearning for relationship, connection, and interconnectedness, which is true to the essence of my soul.

In this same way, the ego derives beliefs and behaviors around strengths that are experienced early in childhood. Whether it is labeled positive or negative, once an experience is embedded in the ego's memory bank, the belief about it becomes reinforced with every new experience that proves it's true.

I have a firm belief that *I am never lost.* This is based on an early story I was told about an incident that happened to me about the age of 2 or 2 1/2. I was separated from my mother in a store in Brooklyn, New York. Not able to find her, I walked down the street and found my way back to my grandmother's house. I was sitting on the stoop feeling quite proud of myself when my mother showed up in a frantic state. I'm not sure what happened next.

My sense is that there was a great relief on the part of my mother and myself. My grandmother was a very wise soul who may have helped my mother put a positive twist on the event. This seems so, because the entire incident instilled a permanent sense of my strength and capability in venturing into new places.

What I do know is that I have an uncanny good sense of direction. I have many experiences that consistently reinforce this belief. At one point, I moved to Delaware, where I became I a public health nurse. With a car, phone book, and map, I was able to find my way around this new territory with no stress and a sense of adventure.

As a result of the early data and ongoing experiences that reinforce it, I firmly believe that *I am never lost, just discovering a new way to get somewhere.* This is a composite inner truth, based partly on my soul's true nature and partly on the ego's formation of a belief that became an embedded pattern (fact). That pattern is intended to protect my life and serve my soul's purpose.

Gary Craig, the developer of the Emotional Freedom Techniques (EFT), talks about the ego structure as the house we live in and our beliefs as the writing on the walls. The writing on our walls is our truth about life and our relationship with it. As adults, with awareness and maturity, we can change the writing on our walls that may hold us back from following our soul's call.

When the soul pushes toward new experiences, the ego tends to push back to maintain the status quo of the original structure. Fortunately, with the right tools, awareness, and understanding, the writing on our walls can be rewritten.

This is important when the soul's passion rises, calling for a transformation of the original structure of the ego-soul relationship. This call of the soul often comes in adolescence, in midlife, or after a significant life shift, like divorce, life-threatening illness, or near -death experience.

The next three chapters will explore all of these concepts along with more detail about the soul, the ego, and other aspects of our psyche that are important to hearing and living the call of your soul.

The following concepts summarize the foundation of the ego–soul journey:

- The soul has both essential qualities common to all souls, plus personal qualities that are unique to your particular soul.

- The soul is has an embodied experience of life.

- The ego evolves out of the physical, sensory experience of the soul.

- The ego and the soul are not separate.

- The ego is also informed by the basic drives for survival.

- The ego reflects qualities of the soul's true nature.

- The ego evolves and reinforces beliefs and behaviors based on early childhood experiences, which are expressed in patterns that become our truth about who we are and how life works.

- It is possible to change our patterns with conscious awareness.

Ideas for Applying This Information to Your Life

Begin to be aware of patterns of belief and behavior that may reflect decisions your ego made based on early life experiences. Get a journal or small tape recorder to note patterns of thoughts, feelings, and actions you observe as you go through the day.

Locate some photos of yourself as a baby or very young child. Then, look at some photos after the age of 7. What changes do you see in the appearance and demeanor of that child at different ages? Can you see more soul qualities at the younger age and more ego influence at the later ages? What qualities of the soul do you see in the young child?

Chapter 2

The Soul

> *Let yourself be silently drawn by the strange pull*
> *of what you really love. It will not lead you astray.*
> —Rumi

What Is Soul?

> *The soul of man is immortal and imperishable.*
> —Plato

We talk about soul music and soul food. What does that
mean? To me, these are unique things that attract each of
us and touch us at a deep level. I call them affinities.

Our specific attractions may change over time, yet we
know them by the way they draw us in and make us feel.
Affinities pull us like a magnet. With that pull, a feeling,
a sensation, arises. It might be delight, lightness of heart,
increased energy, a spark. It's like something just turned
up the inner pilot light a notch.

In energy terms, affinities are on the same wavelength with us. In this way, affinities are clues to our true nature. They are mirrors that reflect our inner light back to us. The source of that light, that attraction, that knowing, is the soul.

Even though we cannot see or touch the soul with our eyes or hands, we can know it directly by how it draws us toward these reflections, these clues. We know how an affinity feels. It's not in our head. It's not logical or rational. We can't always explain why we are attracted to that particular vibration, that particular flavor. It's a matter of taste or comfort. Inside, we just know.

With hindsight, the clues begin to add up. We can see themes and patterns to our affinities. Also, there are usually gifts, talents, and natural abilities that align with our affinities. These are reflections of the personal qualities of the soul that are unique to each individual.

Right from the beginning, even in utero, a mother can tell a difference from one pregnancy to another. This baby may be more active or calm. He might move to a certain type of music. She might respond to the mother's emotions. After birth, we can observe the child's affinities in actions, reactions, preferences, or behaviors.

My first granddaughter hated to sit in her little baby seat. She wanted to be picked up and walked around.

It's as if she couldn't wait to be able to walk. She always wanted to be moving. As she grew up, she was very agile. She loved to climb and move. It's no surprise that in elementary school, gymnastics attracted her attention. She also excelled at it and quickly became a star in her gymnastics troupe. She not only had the affinity, she also had the natural ability to successfully actualize her soul's desire. She loved to perform in tournaments. When she performed, her energy was boundless, her movements were effortless, and her face glowed with delight. This un-self-conscious self-expression is the soul made visible.

The soul's reflection in affinities and abilities is easiest to observe in infancy and early childhood before the ego structure is fully formed. This is especially true when children feel free to express themselves with minimal restriction. Although affinities and abilities are unique aspects of individual souls, there are also aspects that all souls share. Curiosity is a good example.

All infants demonstrate curiosity. It's through curiosity and exploration that a child naturally learns about the world. Maria Montessori based her philosophy of early childhood education on her observation that the natural tendency of children is to learn. When an environment supports the child's natural curiosity and attractions, he or she loves to learn and does this automatically.

Here is another example. I have a picture of myself about age 3, sitting in a big wingback chair with an opened book on my lap. That was a book for my soul. I can still remember fondly the rough texture of the hardback cover, see the bright yellow color, smell the pages, and hear the crack of the spine. At 3, I don't think I could read the book but I looked at it over and over. I carried it everywhere with me. It was called *Not Only for Ducks: The Story of Rain.* This book explained all about how rain operated, how water evaporated, how clouds formed, and how and why the rain came down.

Before the age of reason, I had an affinity for books, and for understanding how and why life works the way it does. My multisensory affinity for and attachment to this book was an early clue to the nature of my soul. Even now, in recalling that moment, I feel warmth in the center of my chest and a sense of comfort and delight having that book with me, even just in memory. It *still* speaks to my soul.

Today, I have a large library of books and often struggle to part with any of them. I tend to give books as gifts and ultimately came to write books. Was my soul calling me to this moment from the very beginning? I would say so.

Qualities of the Soul

> *The growth of the soul may be compared to the growth of a plant. In both cases, no new properties are imparted by the operation of external causes, but only the inward tendencies are called into action and clothed with strength.*
>
> —George Ripley

One of the most powerful and genuinely helpful processes to shape my experiences and understanding of soul is the *Diamond Heart Approach* developed by A.H. Almass. He outlines the essential qualities of true nature or soul as brilliance, clarity, curiosity, compassion, joy, love, peace, strength, truth, value, will, and more. These are not theoretical constructs, but qualities we can know through our direct sensory experience of them.

Through the process of learning to live in a mortal body in the world, we lose touch with our awareness of these qualities before we are consciously aware of them or have language to describe them. The good news is that through a process of awareness and observation, we can reconnect to our experience of these aspects of our true nature as adults.

I have come to deeply appreciate the amazing ability we have as human beings to sense, observe, and reflect on experiences through our body and being. It is a skill that we can learn and use to develop the self-value, esteem, and unconditional love that are essential to living happily in the world.

These qualities of the soul are always available to us, whether we are consciously aware of them or not. Unfortunately, we learn very early in life to control our physical and emotional reactions. Then, we tend to rationalize or intellectualize our experiences to the point that we desensitize ourselves to the promptings of our soul.

I didn't realize until I went into a therapy process after my parents died that I was living almost entirely from my neck up. My entire focus for understanding life was through reading and reasoning. In Western culture, the mind is the master (positive thinking, mind over matter, believe and achieve). This seems useful until you learn that the soul speaks to you through your senses and feelings. There's the rub.

The essential qualities of the soul arise as we need them. When you are aware and attuned to how the soul communicates, you can notice these qualities in yourself and others.

The quality of strength arose as I was working with a coaching client. Mary was sharing how weak she feels every time she tries to defend her wants to others. As she relayed stories about defending her needs, I visibly saw and heard energy drain from her face and voice. I asked her to stop telling the story and *"Tune in to where you are feeling weak in your body and describe how it feels."* I encouraged her to just observe the feelings and describe what she noticed.

Like waves, sensations came up and gradually changed. She felt heaviness in her heart. As she observed that sensation it began to change. She saw a block of coal melt into a puddle of water. Then, tears welled up behind her eyes. As a tear rolled gently down her cheek, she began to notice energy in her feet. She watched the energy move up her legs and into her belly and solar plexus. Suddenly, she felt a sense of strength! Strength is a quality of the soul.

As we reflected on the experience, it became clear to Mary that once she was able to allow her weakness and vulnerability by simply staying present and observing them without judgment, right behind them strength arose. She started to see how strength was actually supporting her continuous attempts to defend her needs to others.

Ultimately, she could see it was her longstanding belief that she couldn't have what she wanted without the approval of others that was keeping her stuck. Once she felt the strength of her soul's support from direct observation and experience, her need for approval from others immediately started to relax.

Heart and Soul

I have put the ear of the soul
In the window of your heart.

—Rumi

Take your finger and point to yourself. Where are you pointing? If you are like most people, you are pointing to your heart. We don't generally point to the head. Even though we give the brain a great deal of respect and value for making our life choices, it is really the heart that guides us to our soul's true desire and purpose.

HeartMath Institute conducts research on the heart and its power in our life. They discovered that the heart actually informs the brain. They did a fascinating study where subjects were shown random images on a screen. Some images were pleasant and others were frightening. HeartMath scientists were able to measure subjects' hearts reacting to frightening images a few seconds before their eyes actually saw the images. The heart *knew* which image was going to be seen before it was viewed.

I have many experiences while driving a car where I suddenly anticipate needing to slow down or change lanes, only to find a few seconds later a deer was about to cross the road or just around a curve a child was riding a bicycle. This research supports my experience that the soul knows what is coming and communicates with us through our heart and emotions.

The brain catalogues past experiences and uses this data for problem-solving, goal-setting, and other functions; it does not have a clue about the future except to speculate about it based on past information. I didn't think about slowing down in the previous example (while driving); I sensed the need to slow down in my body.

It's the soul that holds the template and vision for our unfolding future. When you are alert to how the soul communicates with you, you can better hear and live your soul's call.

Soul Unfolds

> *The unknown is what it is. And to be frightened of it is what sends everybody scurrying around chasing dreams, illusions, wars, peace, love, hate, all that.... Accept that it's unknown, and it's plain sailing.*
>
> —John Lennon

The soul is not goal directed. You cannot see where you are going or the end point to your venture. The soul unfolds moment by moment like a flower. The call of the soul is how the soul prompts you to take the next step in this unfolding process. Our life purpose reveals itself with each unfolding step we take into the unknown.

Your life purpose is not like a goal you work toward or implement. You can only have a sense of your purpose based on hindsight in recognizing the themes and patterns of steps you took. When you recall the choice points in those moments you can begin to see and feel the way your soul calls you.

I can see in hindsight that the way my soul calls me is primarily through other people. On a few rare occasions, after being in prayer or meditation, I also had spontaneous moments of calling. It was through looking at these key moments in my history that I could identify patterns. The first time I observed the patterns was by listing stepping stones in a journaling exercise developed by Ira Progroff.

It was only in returning to look at that exercise recently and adding more stepping stones that I could see how my soul calls me through other people. I also saw that my ego initially resists the call and vacillates for a short time before I take the step forward. Once I finally take the step, the purpose in taking it is revealed.

Here are just a few (of many) stepping stones that illustrate how my soul reveals its purpose through the intervention of other people:

> An English teacher in 10th grade recommended me for a summer class in comparative philosophies and religions. (I call it the "isms" class.) In that class I learned about journaling. In my first journal, I wrote, *All religions say the same thing at their core—Love your creation and Love your neighbor as yourself.*

➤ In my second year of college an instructor urged me to accept a mental health nursing traineeship. It not only paid for my last two years of college along with providing a living stipend, it required me to spend two years working in the mental health field. During my first job in a research unit for autistic children, I learned from the originators of Family Systems Theory how early childhood experiences form the core patterns that guide our life.

➤ In my second job as a public health nurse, a speaker invited me to attend the first Summer Institute on Alcohol Studies, where I met people who changed their lives 180 degrees. I became inspired to learn exactly how people do this.

➤ I was so enthusiastic about what I was learning at the conference that the director of alcoholism services offered me a job that just became available through a grant. The other people hired for this grant along with me created a new field called Employee Assistance Programs (EAPs). This work involved teaching people about stress, which led to forming my own national training and EAP business. That evolved the in-depth understanding of stress that resulted in my first book, *34 Instant Stress-Busters*.

➤ A friend invited me to a freelance writers' conference, where I met a book agent. In talking to that agent at a break, she invited me to submit a proposal to her that resulted in writing this book.

This book is the culmination of knowledge built step by step by saying *"yes!"* to the call of my soul. Those invitations are often delivered through others.

The clues began at age 3 with the attraction to a book on how rain works, and age 9 with the quest to know what life is about and how it works. Since then I've been called through many people on what seemed to be a haphazard path as I was living it.

In hindsight, I can see that the path was not haphazard or disconnected at all. It is an amazingly coherent accumulation of knowledge and experiences needed to write this book, which is just a current step in the ongoing unfolding of my soul's purpose.

When you see the steps of your life as coherent patterns and themes, you can begin to trust the soul's wisdom in guiding how your life unfolds. Once you come to trust that there is a method to the madness in the events of your life, your ego can also begin to learn to trust the soul's unfolding.

Your Unique Blueprint

> *Each person is born with an infinite power*
> *against which no earthly force is of the slightest*
> *significance.*
>
> —Neville Goddard

Like an acorn holds the blueprint for the oak tree, your soul has the template or blueprint for your life. The acorn cannot grow into a pine tree or a birch tree. You cannot be anyone else but your unique self. Your life plan and purpose are within you, in your soul. Looking for who you are or asking someone else what your life purpose might be is pure folly. He or she cannot know.

That said, people who have succeeded in discovering their own soul qualities and purpose may be able to support you in seeing the clues that reveal yours. I feel fortunate to be guided by several gifted teachers, counselors, and coaches through this process.

The patterns of your life, the choice points or stepping stones you experience, are clues to the way your soul calls you to your purpose. You may also get glimpses of your soul's purpose at different times in your life. You may feel called to a place or situation or role, and recognize that you had a clue about that moment earlier in your life.

In a recent women's retreat, one of the women suddenly realized such a moment. As she started describing an image she drew on her vision board, her eyes grew with surprise, saying, *"I remember drawing a blueprint of this same house I now have a vision to build when I was 7 years old."*

One of my clients, who wanted to know her purpose, talked about delighting in gathering neighborhood kids together to play teacher to them as a young child. The one job she remembered loving earlier in her career was precepting (acting as a mentor/teacher) nursing students. I asked her to remember a time when she was mentoring a student and to "tune in" to her feelings as she talked about it. She smiled, her eyes lit up, and her voice became animated and energized as she shared her excitement in that experience.

When you tap into the soul's purpose, you know it! Eyes light up and enthusiasm appears. Enthusiasm comes from the Greek *en* (to be with) and *thios* (the divine). When you get a glimpse of that divine purpose of your soul, it's like turning up your inner pilot light. There is warmth, excitement, passion, and clarity. Your eyes become clear and bright. There is no mistaking that energy.

I'll never forget the dramatic shift in Michael's energy the moment he tapped into his soul's purpose. Michael was referred to me at the age of 21 because he felt depressed, couldn't find any motivation, was experiencing physical pain, and did not have a sense of direction in his life. He had been through the traumatic death of his father and multiple surgeries from a truck accident. His recuperation was slow and painful.

We met for several months, during which I focused on helping him release past trauma and current pain, and reclaim some energy that we could use to begin exploring his future. Then one day, after getting centered, I asked my usual starting question: *"Take your awareness into your heart, Michael. What does your heart desire for this session today?"* After a few moments, he said with conviction, *"Purpose. I want to know what I am supposed to do next."*

I invited him to stay in that inner meditative space and asked, *"If you could do anything you wanted to do and money and time were no object, what would it be?"* His response was clear and to the point: *"I would be an artist."* I prompted, *"And what do you see yourself doing as an artist?"* At this point, a complete vision poured out of him with such energy, clarity, and conviction that I felt transported right into his experience. I could not only see it, I felt the truth of it.

Then I asked, *"What would need to happen to get there?"* His response came instantly: *"I could do it now if I had the money."* I continued, *"What's the next step you need to take?"* He knew and answered, *"I need to go back to school for my masters in fine arts."* I asked, *"Where would you go?"* He instantly named two top universities in the country. *"Okay. Get the applications and send them in,"* I directed.

All of this happened just about as quickly as you were able to read it. Michael did not require long periods of time pondering his answers. He tapped directly into a source within himself that knew the vision for his future with utter clarity.

Once we arrived at the point of action, which involved thinking about sending in applications, the ego mind weighed in on the conversation. Doubts and fears arose about getting into one of these prestigious schools, how much it would cost, and so on.

This is typical. The ego mind has no concept of this future, has no idea how it can happen, and demands to have a plan before proceeding. The soul does not give us a plan; we only have the first step and must trust that the next step will unfold perfectly as we go along.

In the next chapter, you will come to understand that the ego does not maliciously intend to be difficult or stop you from having what you want. Understanding and compassion are keys to successfully hearing and living the call of your soul.

※

The following concepts summarize the nature of the soul:

- The soul unfolds the blueprint of your life moment by moment.

- The themes and patterns of turning points in life are clues to knowing your soul.

- The soul communicates with us through the heart and emotion.

- The soul communicates its knowing with clarity, passion, and enthusiasm.

- The soul provides direction one step at a time.

Explore These Ideas to Get to Know More About Your Soul

Can you find themes in the situations, activities, or other things (tastes, colors, sounds, smells, textures, temperatures, foods, animals, environments) to which you are attracted in your life?

What are the key moments of choice that brought you to where you are now in your life? Can you see patterns or themes in the steps you took or the process you used at each step?

Can you remember moments when you felt you knew what was going to happen next just before it happened?

Chapter 3

The Ego

Our greatest illusion is to believe that we are what we think ourselves to be.

—Henry Amiel

What Is the Ego?

Your task is not to seek for love, but merely to seek and find all the barriers within yourself that you have built against it.

—Rumi

The ego forms as the embodied soul rubs up against experience in the world. The ego is not who you are. It is an image of who you are based on messages you received and impressions of your experiences as a young child.

The first mirrors in which we see ourselves are the eyes of our parents or primary caregivers. As soon as they discovered that you were a boy or girl, they formed expectations of how you would be and who you would become.

As babies and young children, we absorb all of these impressions without exception.

These mirrors are not clear, precise, authentic reflections of our true nature or soul. Each person with whom we interact reflects to us a composite of images made up from what *they* learned and believe. The baby absorbs everything like a sponge. There is no conscious choice involved in what we believe or reject from impressions imposed on us from these distorted mirrors.

It is generally accepted that the foundation of the ego forms by 5 to 6 years old. The "age of reason" is about 7 years old. The ego is not rational or logical from an adult perspective. It is created from the responses and reactions of a naïve child at the precognitive and preverbal stages of development. If you knew the circumstances, the age of the child, and the way the child sees the world, you might understand more clearly how that ego adopted certain beliefs.

Logical arguments against these beliefs will not change them. This is what perplexes and frustrates people who attempt to help others by presenting logical arguments for changing a behavior pattern to no avail. The ego forms through experience, and it is only through having a radically different experience that the ego is able to form a new belief.

Here is a sweet example of how conditioning occurs. I received the following note from a friend, who consistently read a book to her daughter that I gave her when she was born: *Funny thing...last night, Ellie insisted upon reading* Good Night, Moon *before bed. I put her in bed, handed her the book, and then, went to turn on her nightlight. As I did, she opened the book and began to "read" ("read" = reciting from memory) the book without me. It began, "To sweet Ellie, with love and light, Aunt Aila...."* My friend obviously read the inscription I wrote in the book each time she read the book to her daughter.

How will this experience play out in Ellie's later life? We can't know for sure. Perhaps she will always want someone to inscribe the front cover or first page of a book given her as a gift. Or, maybe she will give books to others with her own inscription in them. Or, whenever she meets someone named Aila, she will love them from the start without knowing why.

Early Experience Becomes My Truth

> *Humans evolve through the metabolism of experience.*
>
> —Deepak Chopra

The child is dependent on the parent or guardian to meet basic needs for survival, approval, acceptance, and love. Based upon the parent's responses to the child, the ego forms beliefs and patterns that become the foundation of the child's self-image and self-esteem. This creates the structure of the internal or psychological house we inhabit.

By the age of 7, these patterns are set in place. They run unconsciously, much like a computer operating system. We don't question them; they are our truth about who we believe we are and how we believe the world is in relation to us.

Here is an example. Somewhere in my early development. I formed a belief that if I did not give people what they want, they would not want to have a relationship with me. As soon as I met people, I would try to figure out what they liked and what was important to them, so I could provide something of value to them.

Though on the surface this may sound like an admirable quality, it was actually a form of manipulation. This behavior was not driven by love or desire to serve the other person; it was driven by fear that the other person would not like me or relate with me if I did not give the person something he or she needed.

Another feature of this pattern was hiding my own thoughts, feelings, and needs. This resulted in inauthentic and superficial relationships. Though the relationships were harmonious and pleasant on the outside, my fear was realized anyway. Inside I felt just as alone as if these people didn't relate with me at all.

This belief didn't only apply to personal relationships; it permeated every aspect of my life. When I conducted presentations, for example, I would look at the evaluation forms at the end of a session. On a scale of 0 to 5, with 5 being excellent, I would thumb through the stack of evaluations: 5, 5, 5, 5, and then come to a 4. When I got to the 4 I stopped cold, trying to figure out what this person didn't like. I would go over and over in my head what I could have done differently. Heaven forbid there was a 3—yikes! Threes were horrendous to me.

Needless to say, this attempt to control what people thought of me in my presentation inhibited spontaneous and genuine connection with the audience. Although the presentations were technically excellent, my soul wasn't in them. Once I was able to confront, challenge, and reconstruct this belief, my presentations became much more animated and dynamic.

Today, I feel very present, authentic, and connected with my audiences. I have genuine concern to meet the needs and desires of the people listening to the presentation. Plus, I now realize that, for some people, a three is as good as it ever gets. This is not something I can control by changing me or my presentation.

Wearing a Mask

> *I AM—the two most powerful words in the world, for whatever we put after them becomes our reality.*
>
> —Susan Howson

The ego becomes the mask we wear personally and the way we present ourselves to others. It is contained in all the descriptors that follow the words *I am.*

We might identify ourselves with the roles we play: I am a woman, man, mom, dad, daughter, son, husband, wife, nurse, engineer, social worker, salesperson. It's not only the word, but all the meaning it carries for us and for society. It might be through behaviors with which we identify: I am a procrastinator, always on time, a book worm, a movie buff, a great cook, a gardener, a manipulator, a teetotaler. How about through our affiliations: I am a Catholic, agnostic, spiritual not religious, a card-carrying member of _____. We might identify with our body: I am tall, short, muscular, slim, obese, big-boned, frail, a redhead.

This is why our ego is attracted to taking personality inventories and other assessment tools. They seem to give us more accurate and specific descriptors our ego can use to define us: I am a nine on the Enneagram, an ENTP on the Myers Briggs, and so on. Whether based on research or just made up by someone, our ego seems to love them all. Keep in mind that even the research-based inventories use participants with an ego.

As soon as you meet another person, the assessment begins about who he or she is based on these external indicators. We do this instantly. I'm sure you have heard that the first few seconds we meet someone is the most important. That first impression is the basis for judgments about us by others that can have longstanding implications in all relationships. Like the ego itself, once a conclusion is made, it takes some work to change it.

These first impressions are based on the outer masks we wear, down to clothing, language, accents, and ethnicity. A good friend of mine told me about her experience on a nude beach. She said that once the novelty wore off, the most striking feature of the experience was that there wasn't any way to make a judgment about others based on what they were wearing. Up until that moment, she hadn't realized the impact clothes made on how we approach people and what assumptions we immediately make about them.

As I am writing this, I just remembered a debate I had with a sociology professor when I was a nursing student at Villanova in the late 1960s. He said my simple printed shift dress was a reflection of what society conditioned me to wear. I was adamant that I was wearing what I liked and society had nothing to do with it. He was apparently delighted with my ability to create logical points to defend my position. I have to smile when I think about it now. I got an A in the class, even though I was dead wrong.

One time, I co-led a women's retreat where each of us went out into nature, brought back things that attracted us, and constructed a mask from them. Then, we took some time to reflect on the meanings the mask conveyed and shared that with the group. It was a profound experience. We rarely stop to think consciously about the message and the meaning reflected in who we are expressing through our everyday masks. You might try this activity for yourself. It is self-revealing.

Here is another aspect of masks. When you make a mask from papier-mâché or latex, the general features form from the authentic curvatures of your face. The ego is like this. Whereas it is not an exact duplicate of the soul characteristics upon which it is based, there are elements of your true nature within and beneath the surface of the masks you wear and present to others.

Here is the way I see the ego in relation to the soul that seems to crystallize the difference for my clients. Would you agree that your thoughts and feelings change continuously and that your body has changed radically from birth to the present? Then, these cannot be who you are, because *you* are the same being that came in the original package when you were born.

Anything that changes cannot be you. You are the being who abides through all those changes. Your consciousness unfolds to reveal and express more and more of the authentic self you have always been. The ego categorizes and compares. Your unique soul, on the other hand, cannot be pigeonholed.

Many times people will say they do not feel their age. Chronologically I am 65, yet my sense of my age is more like 45 and the wisdom of my age feels like 95. This also brings to mind a time many years ago when I weighed more than 300 pounds. I was heavily (pun intended) involved in my spiritual life and development. I felt totally light. I could not feel my body's weight or my feet on the ground. Once I started to release the weight, I realized that part of why I gained it was to actually *feel* a sense of embodiment and ground for my spirit.

As we grow in consciousness, layers of the mask can be removed. Sometimes we feel safe to do this with certain select individuals and then with like-minded groups. Fear arises when we reveal more of our true nature to others; it feels acutely risky. The ego remembers the consequences we endured as a child for being our authentic self. When we face the fear and take the risk with an open and accepting person, life-changing freedom is the payoff.

I remember the most life-changing moment for me in removing the mask of rationality in relating to others strictly from my intellect. This mask protected me from the abandonment by others who might be put off by my enthusiasm and expressive energy. At the end of my first week in the *Diamond Heart* group, I finally broke down in pure relief. I didn't speak in the large group all week. That final moment, I stood up and expressed my deep gratitude for the unconditional love and acceptance I felt each time I revealed more of my true feelings and energy. I was in awe that I could actually share the full impact of my excitement and enthusiasm with these people and *no one* left the room. They actually applauded the courage it took to reveal this. Tears are streaming down my face again as I recall the life-changing power of that moment.

Taking the risk to remove portions of our masks is a relief for both the ego and the soul. The ego doesn't have to work so hard to keep up the façade, and the soul gains more freedom of expression in our lives.

Ego Structure

You cannot out-perform your self-image.

—Dr. Maxwell Maltz

Whereas the nature of the soul is free flowing, flexible, and mobile, the structure of the ego is rigid, stable, and defined. I think of the ego as a house constructed to protect the soul and provide security in a world of expectations and rules.

The structure of the ego is rigid. The ego doesn't say, *"Everyone won't like you as you are, so be yourself and just understand that."* No, no, no. The ego is emphatic and often frightening: *"Don't do that again! People will hate you, abandon you, kill you."* It's not like you actually hear these words in your head; it is the feeling of panic you get from the fear that arises when you even *think* about doing something new.

The ego was created to protect the soul and maintain survival of the body that houses it. It takes its job seriously! These are the internal rules we live by to feel secure, accepted, and loved. Any attempt to challenge these structures triggers fear.

This structure, also called "conditioning," serves the soul well through childhood. Conditioning is our acculturation to living safely and successfully in the world. It is functional and cannot be avoided. This is the part that tells us not to burp at the table or talk with a mouth full of food.

Once the ego forms, it is the belief structure within which we live our life. As a result, our life takes on patterns of behavior and experience that reinforce those original beliefs. In this way, ego beliefs become our truth.

You may have heard the term *self-fulfilling prophecy*. Today it is often called the *Law of Attraction*. The principle is this: What you believe and expect is what happens. Not what you consciously believe. You may consciously believe you can have a million dollars, win the lottery, or become an artist, while your unconscious truth says, *"You are a loser who can never have what you really want," "Money doesn't grow on trees,"* or *"You can't draw a straight line."*

We continue to use the same unconscious operating system or structure until something happens that *forces* us to confront and change it. Even in the face of the unhappiness, pain, and suffering our beliefs may cause, we tend to cling doggedly to the structure of security that is familiar to us.

We can see this frequently in dating or marriage patterns. Eloise married two alcoholics. The third time, she purposely selected a man who was a teetotaler in order to avoid that pattern. After three years of marriage, she came to talk with me about her devastating financial situation. As it turned out, this husband developed a gambling problem that drained her savings. It is extremely frustrating to think you found a way to change a pattern through making a conscious choice only to find that the pattern repeats itself anyway.

Here is an example from my own conditioning. I believed I could never have what I really wanted. Even in the face of all the evidence that goal-setting works for many people, I knew that if I set a goal for something I really wanted, I would not get it. In fact, declaring out loud what I wanted to someone would *guarantee* I could not have it.

I have evidence from my childhood of asking my mother for something I had my heart set on and her telling me, quite bluntly, *"You can't have that!"* This happened enough times that I came to see my mother as the pin that burst my balloon. Eventually I stopped asking, because I knew the truth that wanting something was not only futile, but that asking would assure that I would never get it.

As an adult, I occasionally became convinced by something I read or a workshop I attended that I should set a goal and work toward something I wanted. It never worked. Because the unconscious belief was still there overriding any conscious choice I tried to make. Only after going through some major transformational processes, including a re-birthing experience in the desert, was I finally able to visualize something I wanted with success.

Now, I teach people to make vision boards so they can get what they want. I personally manifest a great deal of what I want easily. I even manifest things I didn't know consciously that my soul wants, like the opportunity to write this book. This is my new truth, today.

Even though the ego structure is stable and fairly rigid, it is not unchangeable. Just as the ego forms out of experience, it can change and adjust with new experiences. This does not generally happen without a compelling reason to change and a conscious effort to identify and alter the core of the unconscious pattern.

This House Is Too Small

We lead our lives like water flowing down a hill, going more or less in one direction until we splash into something that forces us to find a new course.

—Chiyo-chan, *Memoirs of a Geisha,*
by Arthur Golden

We usually conform, happily or unhappily, within the confines of the ego house we have built until the walls feel too confining for the soul's purpose. This can happen any time there is a major change in the environment, such as an accident, divorce, death of parents, or a natural disaster, for example. Aside from dramatic or traumatic events, it most typically happens in adolescence and mid-life. There are a couple of reasons for this.

Up until about junior high, we live within the structure of the family and the structure of school. We don't have many options or choices outside of those structures. At about junior high school, someone asks us to consider the roles we might play in the world of work. The question *What do you want to be?* opens the space for the soul to call us to our deepest desire, passion, and purpose.

Unfortunately, the desires of the adolescent are often judged as unrealistic. Their energy is channeled into more education and getting a financially stable or lucrative job. At this point, we are guided to live within additional structures determined by educational institutions and the workplace.

I wanted to go into the Peace Corps from high school. I remember vividly a painful conversation in the kitchen with my parents when I told them my plan. My father was clear that I needed to go to college, and my mother was clear that I should be a nurse. You know what happened from the credentials on this book cover.

There may be some aspects of learning and work that speak to your soul. You know this when you love what you're learning or doing. All too often, though, work is viewed as a daily grind that must be endured until retirement, when you may finally get to do what you really want. We tend to work within this structure until a change occurs in environment, health, or a relationship. Radical change opens space again to explore what your soul really wants.

With dramatic physical and emotional changes in adolescence, the house begins to feel confining, as the soul pushes forward with curiosity. The adolescent asks, *"Who am I?"* and *"What is the purpose of my life?"* Parents and society generally tend to respond with prescribed expectations for how to succeed as an adult. These can include: go to school, get a good job, get married, raise children, and so on. The adolescent can conform or fight against these external societal ideals. Either way, the structure of the house is reinforced.

Conformity brings certain rewards; opposition brings consequences, and the collective ego structure of society remains intact. In order to chart a new, independent path, the structure of the house must be renovated. This can happen in adolescence, though it is rare. Although a desire to follow the call of the soul is strong, it takes a lot of courage, stamina, conviction, and determination to successfully chart a unique path against the forces of social conformity.

It can be done, and there are more role models for this emerging as rapid changes in technology and social norms create space between the cracks in societal structure to allow for personal change. Bill Gates and Steve Jobs, both college dropouts, are examples of successful societal renegades.

The 20-something Millennial generation is at the crossroads of this shift. They are prolonging the adolescent developmental stage into young adulthood as they struggle to make clear choices in a society undergoing radical change.

As the job market shifts, college graduates struggle to find a job. Divorce is the norm. And, for the first time in history, children are predicted to make less money and have a shorter lifespan than their parents. The old social norm of go to school, get a job, get married, and raise children is getting harder for society to uphold as the ideal for success. Today's adolescent needs and often seeks a new model for hearing and living the Call of his or her Soul.

If the call is not followed in adolescence, the next window of opportunity for radical change is at midlife. Once again the soul calls us to question the meaning and purpose for the remainder of our life. This time, we're not struggling against parental expectations; we struggle against maintaining the security of the work and family structures we built ourselves. Often it is an event that seems traumatic at the time (a divorce, a layoff, an illness, a death, or intolerable angst with the status quo) that provides the pressure and space to follow a new, uncharted path.

The ego is all about maintaining safety and security. Predictability and illusion of control in life are supported by structure. The structures of school, work, marriage, and religion all provide standards and rules by which to live. When we live within these rules, we are promised certain benefits. Breaking the rules brings consequences.

Social Change and Structural Challenges

We do not have a fear of the unknown. What we fear is giving up the known.

—Anthony De Mello

In recent years, the illusion of security in social structures is shattering. People work loyally for a company for 20 years, only to be laid off with no benefits. Divorce is the norm, and even with a college education, young adults are struggling to find a job and become independent. The promise of security by saving and investing money was broken by unethical practices on Wall Street. Even with all our technology, we are still challenged in predicting radical weather changes and devastating natural disasters. When personal and social ego structures are challenged like this, fear escalates and stress abounds.

In times like these, many egos cling even more rigidly to old structures. Religious fundamentalism and desires to return to earlier models of the so called "traditional" family created post–World War II are good examples of ego attempts to reinforce old structures to achieve an illusion of security in the face of radical change.

Whereas the ego fears change, our true nature—the nature of the soul—thrives on change and growth. The soul is our ground of being. We can count on the abiding, unfolding soul to know *exactly* how to move through a changing environment.

Moment by moment, the future is unpredictable. Our capacity to feel confident, secure, and independent in a world of change is supported by strengthening our conscious connection to the soul. Anne Morrow Lindbergh said it well: *"Only in growth, reform, and change, paradoxically enough, is true security to be found."*

We cannot do this effectively by rejecting, overriding, or suppressing the ego, as is often recommended in spiritual work. The ego is not separate from the soul, and we are not separate from either of these aspects of our self. The ego evolved in relationship with the soul in order to protect and serve it. To reject the ego is to reject a part of ourselves.

This is the dilemma in spiritual work that views the ego as an enemy rather than acknowledging it as valid and valuable. That is not to say that the young ego, which was formed at the precognitive and preverbal stage of development, is still entirely helpful to us as we become adults. When our soul wants to express itself more fully, this early ego structure painfully inhibits that process. The ego forms and re-forms out of experience, so expanding one's perspective from the limiting beliefs formed early in life requires a more compassionate, experience-based approach than outright rejection.

The purpose of this book is to offer you a framework and strategies to support you at every stage of life to live more fully, happily, easily, and successfully through knowing how to hear and live the call of your soul. This also requires knowledge and skill in how to renovate the original structure of the inner house built through the partnership of the ego and soul.

Before we move on to explore the processes for change, there are two more elemental aspects of our psyche that must be addressed. These are the "enforcer," often called the inner critic or superego, and the non-judgmental, curious "observer." We will explore these aspects in the next chapter.

><

The following concepts summarize the nature of the ego:

- The ego's purpose is to protect and serve the soul.

- The ego evolves as the soul has life experiences from 0 to 5 or 6 years of age.

- The ego is not based in logic and reason.

- The ego forms beliefs that you eventually claim as your truth.

- Ego patterns are observed in repetitive life experiences.

- The ego is the basis for self-image and self-esteem.

- The ego is not who you are; it is a reflection of the true nature of the soul in combination with evolved beliefs about who you are and how the world works.

- The ego protects your true identity from you and others through the masks you use to define and express yourself.

- The ego has an original structure that can be re-structured during times of radical change or choice.

Explore These Questions to Get to Know Your Ego Better

What masks do you wear with your friends?

What masks do you wear when you meet someone new?

What masks do you wear professionally in your work?

What masks do you wear in relationships with significant others in your life?

How is your ego trying to protect you by using these masks?

Chapter 4

The Enforcer and Observer

The higher self gets curious. The conditioned self gets defensive.

—Paul and Layne Cutright

Two's Company, Three's a Crowd

The fish trap exists because of the fish. Once you have the fish, you can forget the trap.

—Chuang-Tzu

In this chapter, we will explore two additional aspects of the self that are important to understand in resolving inner conflict and supporting the call of your soul. I call these aspects the enforcer and observer.

In self-development literature, the enforcer is often referred to as the inner critic or judge; Freud called it the superego. Some people lump it together with the ego and call both the ego. I call it the enforcer, because I've come to see its role as specific and separate from the ego. It enforces the structure created by the ego and soul in their early relationship by using both positive and negative self-judgment.

Although the ego is essential to living an embodied life, when it comes to the enforcer in the mature ego-soul relationship, three's a crowd. Once you grow up and become conscious about the value of structure in your life, the enforcer's job is obsolete. It can and must be eliminated to achieve inner peace of mind.

The observer, often known as the higher self, is completely non-judgmental. Its nature is curiosity. This feature of our consciousness is vital to supporting the expansion and renovation of the ego structure to allow more space for the soul to unfold. It is important to strengthen the observer, which increases self-awareness, understanding, and wisdom.

The Enforcer

If you want to reach a state of bliss, then go beyond your ego and the internal dialogue. Make a decision to relinquish the need to control, the need to be approved, and the need to judge.

—Deepak Chopra

The ego contains the rules about life and how we must act to live safely in the world. The enforcer feels like the whirring siren and flashing red light of the police officer following you. Its purpose is to enforce the ego rules. It intimidates, manipulates, scares, or downright terrorizes you into obeying the rules. It constantly reminds you of the consequences of stepping out of line.

Often the enforcer uses the actual words and tone of voice of a parent or primary caregiver from your childhood. You may hear these words as an ongoing criticism in your head, which constantly analyzes everything you do and say. *"Oh my G––, I can't believe you said that! What's wrong with you? Your sister would never have been that stupid."*

We usually think of the critic as negative, yet it contains positive reinforcement as well. The enforcer may pat you on the head as if to say *"Good boy"* or *"Yes, you finally did it right that time."* Whether the assessment is that you are good or bad, it is still a judgment based on the original rules under which the ego formed.

Many of the comments come under the category of "should": *You should be more organized* or *You should have known better than that* or *You shouldn't think that way.* It is important to be alert to how your mind attempts to control your behavior with these messages.

Here's a tip: Start to be alert to the word *should* in your mind and in your language. When you hear it, stop. Ask yourself: *Who made that up?* or *Where did that idea come from?* There are only a few laws of nature; the rest of the rules are made up by human beings.

Some of the rules, like stopping at a red light, are useful. If a "should" seems useful to you to maintain civilized functioning in a world with other people, then keep it and eliminate the judgmental tone behind it. Your ego already knows these useful rules. You don't need the enforcer to constantly remind you of and beat you up over the consequences. The constant judgmental chatter of the enforcer is a major barrier to hearing and living the call of your soul. It must be addressed.

Everyone has a unique version of the enforcer. Some are hostile and abusive; mine was manipulative. If I had a meeting with people, it would start in the shower. *Jim is quiet; he might be intimidated by you. You know how you intimidate men. You better watch what you say. You should just be quiet and not speak up so much....* This anticipation of what people might say and do, and how I should respond went on and on. The enforcer kept my mind busy going through every possible scenario with scripts for me to use in each one. Of course, this eroded any iota of trust I might have in my ability to handle whatever came up.

Getting dressed took forever, as the enforcer judged each item according to how people might judge me: *"Everyone will be wearing suits; you better put on a jacket,"* or *"Oh, that doesn't look very good; you need to lose a few pounds before you wear that again...."* After the meeting, it would analyze everything I did and said in relation to how people might be thinking or feeling about it. Notice that this enforcer is emotionally stuck at about junior high level. It's all about me and how I fit in the world according to how my peers judge me.

One of my clients, Paul, has an enforcer that undermines his thoughts and feelings to the point that he can never trust his choices as "good enough." He has a huge library of books and is always looking for the guru with the "right" answer. (*Well, Dr. Joseph says... but then, you tell me.... and then I read somewhere that....*) This is very effective in keeping Paul stuck, so he doesn't move out of the comfort zone of the ego structure.

These are the overt judgments. There are also covert judgments. Based on these judgments, we hide parts of our selves that are unacceptable. These characteristics are not only hidden from others, but we also hide them from our own awareness. You can become more aware of these deeply hidden self-judgments by being alert to the judgments you make about others.

Projection

> *We meet ourselves time and again in a thousand disguises on the path of life.*
>
> —Carl Jung

You've heard the expression "When you point the finger at someone else, three more fingers point back at you."

We cannot see in someone else a characteristic we don't have some reference for within our self. Whether you see something you either love or hate in another person, that person is just serving as your personal movie screen. He or she displays back to you something your own projector is casting onto him or her. That's why this tendency is called projection.

I remember my first rude awakening to this concept. I was at a conference complaining about how someone's anger was creating a disruption. The presenter looked me right in the eye and said, *"So you must be pretty angry yourself."*

"I'm not anything like that person," I protested.

His response stopped me cold: *"You can't see what you don't have."* I was silent for a long while as I thought about this.

Until that moment, I believed there was no anger, hatred, or malice in me *at all.* My self-image included being accepting of others, a peace lover, and someone who lets things roll off her back. I didn't feel or express anger—ever. "They"—people who are angry—are nothing like me. This is the power of the enforcer. It can keep us completely in the dark about normal aspects of human nature that do not fit the self-image, the mask, our ego chose for us to wear.

Another powerful experience with projection was in my first therapy session when I was describing how there were only three people in my life who frustrated me. The therapist asked, *"What do they have that you want?"*

My first thought was: *"They don't have anything I want. I can't imagine wanting to be anything like them."* Once I stopped personalizing the reaction, I could step back and see that all of these people said and did whatever they wanted with no regard for how other people felt they had to accommodate those whims. I felt constantly challenged to maintain a good relationship with each by being the ultimate accommodator. It took a few minutes to go beneath the surface and see what they had that I deeply wanted. Then, I finally saw it: they each had the confidence and freedom to be their self at any cost!

When you hear yourself saying "they" or "them," as a way of distinguishing the difference between others and yourself, this is a good place to look for the self-judgment of the enforcer. Strong reactions to others are projections, which reflect an aspect of yourself that you are afraid to acknowledge and own. In order to have an open, honest, loving relationship with yourself, you must learn to embrace all of you, even the parts you were taught are "bad" or "ugly."

The most profound and powerful wisdom I ever heard about self-acceptance of these unacceptable aspects of the self came from Maya Angelou at a conference. Someone asked her what she thought about forgiveness. She said, *"I think forgiveness is an arrogant position. I have come to realize that, as a member of the human species, whatever one of our species is capable of doing, we are all capable of doing, including murder, rape, lying, stealing. The reason I do not do these things is that I had the good fortune to have a loving grandmother and a good education. I have other options."*

You and I are human. Given the right circumstances I know today, I can lie, steal, become enraged, and be selfish, for starters. Carl Jung called the parts of yourself that you are afraid to own the "shadow."

Hiding in the Shadow

You gain strength, courage, and confidence by each experience in which you really stop to look fear in the face. You are able to say to yourself, 'I have lived through this horror. I can take the next thing that comes along.'

—Eleanor Roosevelt

You can run, yet the harder you run, the more you find you cannot really hide. What you most strongly deny in yourself will eventually come up to bite you. We see the shadow exposed every day in our culture.

The celibate priest denies and suppresses his human sexuality, then is exposed as a pedophile. There are countless preachers who denounce immorality, only to have their illicit affairs exposed. And who can forget the famous presidential acclamation by Richard Nixon, *"I am not a crook,"* before resigning in disgrace due to the Watergate scandal?

These are extreme examples of the enforcer at work. The harder you try to deny and suppress your humanness, the more it becomes exposed. In this dynamic, we see a law of nature revealed: What you resist, persists!

Shame and Guilt

> *To gain that which is worth having, it may be necessary to lose everything else.*
>
> —Bernadette Devlin

The ego structure and the enforcer judgments are all based in past experience. Some of those experiences are so powerfully imprinted that it seems they can never be reconciled or released. Guilt and shame fall into this category. Whether the gravity of a situation is minor or major is not relevant; the emotional impact of guilt or shame is the same.

Guilt is a judgment that you did something wrong and often comes with a belief that you must pay the price for it. I heard a war veteran say, *"I don't deserve to be happy or have a happy family since I am guilty of taking someone else's family away."*

I carried tremendous guilt around most of my life for looking at a classmate's paper during in a test in fifth grade. I stole an answer. I cheated. I kept the secret, never telling anyone or paying a price for it. The guilt gnawed at me at various times in my life, until I finally released it. Even though the gravity of this situation seems minor in comparison to the first example, each person carries a burden of guilt affecting their self-image.

Rather than the guilt that I did something wrong, shame is the judgment that there is something wrong with me. I am the problem, or I am defective. Shame means "to cover." Feeling ashamed is the need to hide or cover a part of you.

At the age of 4 or 5, Sara was watching her dad feed his pigeons and noticed the eggs in the nest. He explained to her that these would hatch into baby pigeons. At dinner that evening, she made a brilliant connection with what she learned that day by saying, *"What if you laid us, Mom?"* Her mother reacted with horror. The shame was so instant that Sara can't remember exactly what her mom said. Yet, the feeling that *there is something inherently wrong with me* caused Sara to hide her insights from others for many years.

Addictions of all kinds are often attempts to alleviate the stress caused by the self-judgment of guilt and shame. The 12-step process of anonymous programs (such as

Alcoholics Anonymous, Overeaters Anonymous, and so forth) is successful partly because it incorporates a way to effectively address and release these self-judgments.

Retiring the Enforcer

The key to change...is to let go of fear....

—Roseanne Cash

Acknowledging, confronting, and retiring the enforcer must occur before you can effectively restructure the ego and follow your soul. When you hear the critical "should" in your mind, notice it, see the judgment in it, identify where it originated in your history, and tell it outright that you no longer need its service. I used to confront my enforcer with *"Thank you for sharing. I've got this now."* The more you do this, the quicker you will notice these judgmental messages and the faster you will eliminate them.

While the ego is essential to life in the body, once you are a mature adult, you do not need self-judgment to keep you in line. Give the enforcer a retirement party and send it on its way.

Keeping secrets from your awareness takes a lot of energy. Being able to acknowledge all of your humanness is, paradoxically, completely freeing. Freeing the judgments of the enforcer allows the ego to free up the old structure, which allows space for the soul to actualize its purpose with less resistance and stress. This also gives you full access to the truth of your nature and the full range of choices available to you.

When the ego structure and the enforcer are strong, they limit your freedom to choose. You are restricted to either choices within what is acceptable, or you can choose the opposite position and take the consequences. This is the limitation of conditioning. We only know what we learned and the opposite. When your mind presents you with options it's *either* I have to do this *or* I am stuck with that, when you can only think of two opposite options, this is a clue that you are stuck in your conditioning.

Peter presents a good example of this principle. In his first session with me, he said, *"I just need to know which decision is right. Put up with her constant criticizing and complaining or get a divorce."* He had no idea there might be other options.

As we explored the possibilities, he could not see himself doing any of them. Even though he realized that other people managed to make different choices, he could not see *himself* making another choice. This is the nature of conditioning. Once we released some of the emotional mortar keeping the structure in place, Peter was free to look at the situation from another perspective.

I recall my first session with my therapist. By the end of the hour, I knew that my marriage was not working and a split was is my future. On the way out the door, I said, *"So, do I get a divorce?"*

My very wise therapist replied, *"Why do you have to do anything?"* It took another seven years working through many issues before it was the right time to make that decision. At that point, my husband and I were able to mediate an amicable closure to our relationship. We untied the knot. That was an option I never considered possible before.

Once judgments are released, you can more freely observe your thoughts, feelings, sensations, and behaviors with curiosity and self-acceptance. This is the doorway to true freedom of choice and trust in your soul's direction.

The Observer

> *I exist as I am, that is enough,*
> *if no other in the world be aware I sit content,*
> *and if each and all be aware I sit content.*
>
> —Walt Whitman

One of the unique features human beings have is the ability to reflect on ourselves. We can observe our experience, our feelings, thoughts, and behaviors. When we make these observations, there is no judgment about them. The observer is like a dispassionate scientist. It just notes the facts of the situation with interest in its purpose or usefulness. The observer's favorite comment is *"That's interesting."*

This aspect of the self is highly valuable in being able to observe the ego structure along with patterns of belief, behavior, and emotion imbedded in that structure. We must be able to see our patterns and appreciate them before we can decide to change them. The observer is vital to the transformation process.

The observer and the enforcer are two separate aspects of what we call self. Unfortunately, as long as the enforcer is in place, as soon as an observation is made, the enforcer is right there to make a judgment about it. In this way, these two aspects become intertwined and appear to be one unit—that is, until we consciously learn how to separate them.

The more you strengthen the observer, you eventually realize that there is nothing unacceptable within yourself. All the aspects of human nature exist; they just are what they are. The more you notice and register awareness of them in your mind rather than wasting energy denying them, the more accurate information you have upon which to formulate your beliefs and make new choices.

Diet and exercise are areas in my life that provide good examples of the impact of the enforcer and value of the observer in making a change. Keep in mind the enforcer sounds very much like a judgmental parent. I would observe that my body is feeling sore and immediately get the message *"You should go to exercise."* Right behind that thought, my inner adolescent would respond, with her hands defiantly on her hips, *"Try and make me!"*

If I went to exercise, it felt like Mom was forcing me to do something against my will. If I didn't go, I would feel the judgment of being guilty and weak-willed. This pattern repeated through most of my life, until I learned how to release the enforcer.

Once the enforcer was out of the way, I could make a conscious choice without all the inner emotional conflict and drama. I went to exercise with my observer engaged. I observed how I felt while exercising. I was free to observe what I enjoyed about it and the kinds of exercise I didn't enjoy. In this way, I was able to choose a program that I enjoy tremendously.

Now, I go to exercise because I enjoy the activity and the after-effects of strength and mobility in my body, rather than from obligation or opposition to an authority who thinks I "should."

We are so used to self-judgment that in the beginning you may need someone to hold the space for or model learning non-judgment. Once you have the new experience, your ego eventually registers the outcome of that experience, and then it can support having that experience more often, because it serves your body and therefore your soul. This is an example of how the ego can restructure.

Value of Observation

> *What am I called to in a day's time? What are the observations I can make regarding my own nature? And, then, as we go we may begin to see some possibilities past our up-til-now seeing.*
> —Dianne M. Connelly

After several sessions with Carol where I encouraged her to stay with and observe her feelings, and experience and how they transform with non-judgmental observation, she said, *"I feel so much more at peace and am wondering what that's about. This is not usually me. What is wrong; life is so much easier."*

Carol became aware of how strengthening the observer shifted her awareness to see herself in a new way which she experiences as "much more peaceful." Her remarks refer to feeling like something is missing. What's missing is the enforcer!

The enforcer dropped away and acceptance strength-ened for observing whatever response arises without judgment. Carol had a strained relationship with her son for many years. When she met him recently, the observer allowed her to be open to feedback from him. She was amazed that she was not defensive as she would have been before and was much more open to what he had to say. Even when he made an acute observation about her, she was able to see his point. This improved the openness in that relationship. Her son felt good about himself and her openness to hearing what he wanted to say.

What is important in this example is the ease with which Carol moves through these experiences with a sense of peace. There is no effort in observing. Once she practiced releasing the enforcer judgments and strength-ening her observer, these functions became effortlessly automatic. When the rewarding results are recognized, that reinforces the process. This becomes a new structure or pattern of living.

Marilyn's experience after strengthening the observer included being able to discern whether self-disclosure was useful or not in a situation. The presence of the observer supports you to be more present in a situation. *When I am in a social situation, I may feel open to say whatever I think without judgment from the others or I may intuit that they are not ready to hear what I have to say. It would not make me stupid if I did say something, yet I feel it is not necessarily welcomed by this group.* Marilyn reported these observations in a matter-of-fact way; there was no emotion involved in the observations. She is free to choose based on what is happening in the moment.

These experiences illustrate an important inner relationship shift: When you acknowledge the wisdom you gain by observing yourself, the ego can relax its protector role, because you, the adult, are assessing the security and safety in a situation. Then, the enforcer drops away because it's not needed to keep you in line like a child anymore.

You can be authentic in being your true self and also wise in scoping the environment to see whether expressing everything you are thinking is necessary or useful. It's not like when we were encouraged to be assertive in the 1970s. When people would say, *"I'm going to be myself no matter what!"* that was more aggressive. This is more like *"I can be myself to myself—and whether I share that with another is my conscious choice in this aware moment."* This is acting from your mature self being present.

It's not that there are no rules—more that the rules are not rigid; they are appropriate to the situation. When you stay with observing an experience, it metabolizes and adjusts. You digest it. You release what is no longer needed and keep the wisdom from the experience.

One of my friends, a marvelous gardener, calls it "tending the inner garden." This metaphor reminds me of how I observed and built a garden when I was going through a major growth period. I felt so restless and confined being indoors for even 30 minutes. So, I took to sitting on the back porch and observed nature in the yard for hours at a time.

I would plant something and then observe how it grew in relation to the things around it. I went through this process for about a year, observing and building a garden consciously, one plant at a time. After this, I wrote several articles about how nature mirrors human life and relationships using the wisdom gained from that experience. I still get feedback from people about the profound insights they gain from reading those articles.

A strong observer is one of the keys to achieving peaceful presence in your life. It also supports the shifts required in the ego-soul relationship to facilitate hearing and living the call of your soul.

❊

The following concepts summarize the nature of the enforcer and observer:

❧ The enforcer enforces ego boundaries using positive and negative self-judgment.

- The enforcer is not needed and must be released once we are mature adults.

- You project onto others aspects of yourself you are afraid to own.

- What you most strongly deny in yourself will surface eventually in damaging ways.

- Having a curious, non-judgmental observer is vital to freedom of choice.

- When you can only see two opposite choices, you are stuck in conditioning.

- A strong observer is one of the keys to achieving peaceful presence in life.

Explore These Ideas to Get to Know More About Your Enforcer and Observer

Begin to notice and journal the negative and positive judgments from the enforcer in your mind. Are there patterns and themes to these judgments? What tone of voice does the enforcer use? Do you recognize the voice as a parent or powerful judge in your life?

Observe how often you hear and use the word *should*. Who made up these judgmental beliefs?

This Mindfulness Exercise can help you strengthen the observer. Take your time with each step: Get one raisin. Hold it between your thumb and forefinger, and just observe its color texture, shape, and contours. Smell the raisin. Then put it into your mouth without biting or chewing it. Just observe how your tongue and teeth move the raisin around. What is the taste and texture of the raisin before you bite into it? Be curious about how you are interacting with the raisin. Observe your thoughts and feelings, as well as the sensations. Bite into the raisin. How would you describe the taste? Which teeth actually did the biting? Notice how the raisin moves in your mouth as you chew it. Swallow the raisin. Can you feel it going down your throat?

How was this exercise for you?

What did you learn about seeing from the observer perspective?

Part II
Hearing and Living the Soul's Call

To grow, you must be willing to let your present and future be totally unlike your past. Your history is not your destiny.

—Alan Cohen

My intention for my clients and for you is that you come to love yourself and the magical mystery of your soul's unfolding, that you will come away from this part of the book with a sense of curiosity in wanting to learn more about your own uniqueness and a sense of awe in the amazing being you are and are becoming, and that you come away with a sense of confidence that it is possible for you to transform your life to have more of what you want.

The wisdom and actualization of my soul's purpose seemed illogical and mysterious as it unfolded. It was a deep desire and curiosity to know the truth and an inner pull to say "yes" that enabled me to trust in the guiding force that continuously offered opportunities for learning and ultimately for wisdom.

Exploring the journey again through my clients' experiences and stepping back to view the seemingly disconnected mosaic of my own experiences, I am able to understand how the journey into an enlightened life unfolds through a loving dance between the ego and the soul. In Chapter 5, I will share how I came to see my ego and soul as partners rather than adversaries.

This is a journey toward knowing the evolving truth while not knowing the outcome. This can be disconcerting to the ego mind, which feels more secure with a destination and a plan. There are ways to allay ego fear of the soul's unfolding process. In Chapter 6, we will look at the process of transformation and how to renovate the ego structure to create more space for the soul to unfold.

Chapter 7 offers ways to hear the call of your soul, and discriminate between the call of the soul and the ideas of the ego. We will also talk about expecting and handling the ego resistance to change, as well as ways to empower your soul's vision.

Our training ground for observing and transforming the ego-soul relationship is real-world experience. Chapter 8 shares examples of how to live this ego-soul relationship in the world of work and interpersonal relationships.

Chapter 5

The Ego and the Soul: A Love Story

> *Continuity gives us roots; change gives us branches, letting us stretch and grow and reach new heights.*
>
> —Pauline R. Kezer

An Inner Love Story

> *We grow partially. We are relative. We are mature in one realm, childish in another. The past, present, and future mingle and pull us backward, forward, or fix us in the present. We are made up of layers, cells, constellations.*
>
> —Anais Nin

The dance of your life is expressed through the intimate relationship between your ego and soul. My intention in this chapter is to help you feel more appreciation and love for your entire journey in this life, even the parts through which you struggle. I've come to understand the ever-changing relationship between the ego and the soul as a beautiful inner love story. Like any love story, this one has trials, tribulations, and triumphs!

This love story begins with the ego's devotion to the soul's protection. The ego loves the soul and the body that houses it. It starts out in the relationship with a mission to protect both from physical, emotional, and psychological pain. The ego learns from life experiences through the physical senses.

In the beginning, the soul and ego work together to build a structure of protection for the young, naïve soul. The baby is a curious, sponge-like being, who learns about the world he or she is born into by downloading experiences through all the senses. What the baby sees, hears, tastes, smells, and feels become part of a vast memory database that forms the foundation of the original ego structure. This is the structure of your beliefs about yourself and your life.

As the soul rubs up against the physical world in infancy and childhood, the young mind evolves a complex of beliefs, which become the foundation for the story we tell about ourselves and life. This original story is formed from the perceptions of a child before the age of reason and meaningful language. Even so, we don't update or change this view until something significant happens that prompts us to change it.

Adolescence, midlife, and life-changing experiences that call into question our identity, such as illness, accidents, divorce, and loss of job, are the kinds of significant changes that spark the deeper questions *Who am I?* and *What is my life about?* It's during these times that a window of opportunity opens to update and change the original perspective and structure by which we live our lives.

The ego begins to take the lead early in the relationship. It continues to structure the dance patterns until the maturing soul feels the need to express itself more and take full charge of directing your life's purpose. As the soul matures, the classic dance of conformity cannot provide enough space and freedom for the soul's unique authentic expression.

These are moments when the soul is ready to create its own dance. Unfortunately, as the soul attempts to step out of the old pattern, its toes get stepped on by an ego that is still trying to maintain the original pattern of protection they formed in childhood. The soul pushes against the walls of the ego structure, which feel too small and confining.

The ego is afraid. It remembers, in vivid detail, all the experiences of pain, frustration, devastation, abandonment, and rejection that the soul felt in the early days as it naively moved out into the world in open innocence. In its effort to protect the soul from the certain consequences that it knows will come from moving authentically again, the ego becomes even more determined to stop the soul.

We feel this ego-soul struggle for leadership as a terrible inner conflict or battle. I called it my "Armageddon" of the soul. The soul wants more freedom, and the ego is determined to keep it safe.

This inner conflict causes stress on a deep, unconscious level. Depending on the unique defense mechanisms the ego developed for protection, our symptoms of stress can include:

➤ Flight: loss of energy and motivation, distraction, procrastination, stress, depression, hopelessness, helplessness, despair.

➤ Fight: anxiety, bullying, complaining, blaming, anger, rage, panic attacks.

➤ Freeze: chronic illness, chronic pain, autoimmune conditions.

We may use any number of methods to deal with the pain of these symptoms, including:

➤ Distraction: television, video games, work, gambling, co-dependence.

➤ Escape: changing residence, relationships, appearance.

➤ Control: obsessive behaviors, possessiveness.

➤ Numbing: alcohol, drugs (including medication), food, sex.

Resolution of the conflict requires the ego to realize that the soul is no longer as naïve, young, or inexperienced as it was in the beginning and that the continued survival of the body and soul no longer requires vigilant protection. What the mature soul now needs from the ego is renovation of the original structure to support growth and change toward unfolding its fullest expression. With a supportive attitude and the right tools, the ego is capable and willing to do this. I know, because I have experienced this inner transformation.

This is not the typical view of the ego. The ego is more often seen as the villain in this relationship and especially in this conflict. We are encouraged in most spiritual practices to take sides in the battle. Of course, we want to be on the side of the soul, our true self, and our soul's purpose. That's why most of the advice we get is to suppress, override, or try to extinguish the ego. I think this is precisely what keeps us stuck. Fortunately, I learned another way that I am delighted to be able to share with you.

Hating or rejecting the ego is self-destructive, because the ego is not separate from you. It is an integral part of the ego-soul relationship. These partners cannot divorce, and the ego cannot move out of the house. The only hope for inner peace is to support the partners to reconstruct and rebalance the relationship in a new way. The ego must be understood and approached with an attitude of appreciation and compassion for the important and loving role it plays in the relationship.

Freeing the Soul

Your breath touched my soul and I saw beyond all limits.

—Rumi

After a few sessions with my therapist, I had a profound, life-changing moment, which forms the cornerstone of understanding this soul-ego love story.

At that point in my life, I had no idea who I was. All I felt was a sense of emptiness, nothingness inside. I had no preferences at all; I could relay all the events and details of my life, yet I couldn't identify anything that created a spark in me. I couldn't even tell you my favorite ice cream flavor. There was no point in having a preference, because there was no way to have what I wanted. I was such an accommodator that I called myself "the chameleon"; I could become anything you need me to be. *"I like what you like."*

My therapist guided me to place my attention into the black space I felt in my core: *"Just stay there and observe what happens."* For a while nothing happened. Then, out of the darkness I started to see something emerge. It looked like a small treasure chest. As it got closer, I could see it was an elaborately carved and jeweled golden

Egyptian sarcophagus. My curiosity rose. He guided me to open the sarcophagus. Inside was what looked like the charred remains of an infant. I began to cry. *"The baby is dead."* I cried with such deep grief for the loss of this baby.

When the tears subsided, he guided me to send love from my heart to the baby. A light beamed from my heart to the charred remains of the baby, completely enfolding and embracing it with light. The baby began to change. It slowly filled out and turned pink. Within a few minutes the baby looked like a beautiful, healthy, fully alive cherub with its arms raised up toward me. Now, I cried with joy! *"The baby is alive!"*

I felt ecstatic and completely alive myself! The emptiness and darkness were gone, replaced by warm golden fullness in my solar plexus. I am still amazed by the instant, permanent internal shift of this experience. I left the therapist's office that day knowing something significant just happened that would change my life in ways I couldn't imagine. I felt like a weight lifted off me—complete relief.

Looking at this experience today, it reflects several features that are significant to the nature of the ego-soul relationship. The ego protected the soul, the essence of the baby, as a treasure in a beautiful, elaborately bejeweled sarcophagus, one that would house a king or queen. This speaks to the preciousness of the soul to the ego. It also disguised the baby to appear dead. What a brilliant way to keep this baby safe. Lastly, the ego still sees the soul as a naïve infant, even though time has passed and the child is now an adult. This is how I understand the true intention of the ego structure and the lack of awareness in the ego of the need to update that structure.

Unfortunately, that structure keeps the essence of the soul so hidden there is no way to express itself. I lived my life entirely to please my parents. During the year after they both died, I felt like an orphan with no direction, no purpose, no feeling, no preferences; I was in limbo. I wondered, *"Who do I live my life for now?"*

Every time I thought about getting help, I couldn't think of anyone who felt like the right person. In my work as an employee assistance counselor, I knew all the counselors and therapists in the city to whom I referred my clients. Many were quite good, yet I had no sense that any of them could help me.

Then one day, an acquaintance, totally unaware of my dilemma, began telling me about her therapist. It was a strange conversation for several reasons. First, I was surprised that she chose to share such an intimate part of her life with me without any prompting or context for it. Second, it's hard to believe that I never heard of her therapist, who worked in the same small city where I referred people to therapists for many years. Most importantly, as I listened to her, I had an immediate sense that I wanted to call for an appointment, even though I had no information about this person.

Elements of Change

> *To accept that absolutely everything Life brings is a gift for your benefit and highest good, is to accept Paradise as a state of mind.*
>
> —Dorothy Mendoza Row

The story I just shared with you illustrates three elements I notice consistently in the organic process of the call of the soul for change: waiting, timing, and knowing.

There are times when life seems to be moving along in a wonderful way when suddenly everything stops and nothing is happening. The first couple of times this occurred I started scrambling for what I was supposed to do that I wasn't doing.

Eventually, I came to call the slack times between growth cycles "waiting periods." It seems there are moments when the previous growth is complete and the timing is not yet right for new growth to begin. Either that, or it is some kind of inner gestation period.

There is a model for this pattern in nature. It's the dormant winter before a new spring. The trees look dead on the surface while underground the roots are being nourished for new growth. That year of limbo after the deaths of my parents was a waiting period.

Then, when the timing is right, a catalyst appears, seemingly out of nowhere, to stimulate the next movement. These are serendipitous moments that mark turning points in life.

As soon as my friend started to tell me about her therapist, I had an inner sense of knowing I wanted to make an appointment. Even though I had no knowledge of his credentials or competency, I *knew* intuitively in my heart he was the one I needed to see. This is an example of the kind of feeling that comes when the soul knows the next step.

Although these elements seem intangible and even magical, they are consistently present throughout life. When your observer is awake and aware, and you allow the call of your soul to take the lead, you begin to see patterns in the way your soul calls you to dance your life in a new way.

This story also highlights the value of a skilled teacher with effective tools and techniques in the transformation process. A truism applies in these situations: when the student is ready, the teacher appears.

From Protector to Server

The eyes are here for seeing, but the soul is here for its own joy.

—Rumi

Through a transformational change process, the ego begins to renovate the original structure to allow more space and movement for the soul. The ego's role shifts from being strictly a protector to serving the soul's unfolding. This involves considerable effort and usually happens gradually.

The ego must build trust in the soul's capability to lead in order to ease up on the belief the soul still needs protection. This is a process of testing and registering the outcome of new experiences. The ego learns through experience. As you risk following the soul's promptings, have a new experience and register thoughts and feelings of happiness, joy, love, and more, the ego restructures to say, *"Okay, we can do that again."*

My earlier example of risking expressing myself fully in the *Diamond Heart* group and experiencing the embrace of surprise, delight, and love when no one left the room is a great example of taking a risk and having a new experience. A short time after that experience, I was invited to test this again with a local Unity congregation. I prepared my talk, and brought notes and books as references for what I planned to present. Then, when I rose to speak, I put all the materials aside and began to speak authentically from my heart.

The old consequences did not happen. People laughed at my humor, and some had tears in their eyes when I told a personal story to illustrate a point. In the end, many told me how deeply that presentation touched them. A few said, *"That was just what I needed to hear today!"* Again, my soul's authenticity and safety in expressing it was affirmed. I consciously noticed and celebrated that moment, which registered the experience in detail with the ego mind.

It took a few more experiences like this before the fear of abandonment that kept the original ego structure in place dropped away completely. It's not there anymore. I know that because I am writing this book from that same authentic place, with no fear, a feeling of open-hearted love, and a sense of trust that this message is the one I am here to share.

I'm prompted to tell you this is not a fluke. I am not special or unusual. You, too, have this capacity and capability. The essence of Maya Angelou's words echo this truth: *"...whatever one of our species is capable of doing; we are all capable of doing."*

Call and Capability

> *Desire is pure potentiality seeking manifestation. Inherent in the desire is the technology for fulfillment.*
>
> —Deepak Chopra

This brings me back to Michael's story. Michael was able to tap into his passion for making a unique form of art, which would take him to study with indigenous people in various parts of the world. In order to do this, his first step involved going back to school, and he knew in his heart which school he wanted to attend. The ego showed no resistance until the point of taking the first step: applying to school. That's when the doubts and fears arose.

Michael used several techniques I shared with him to release the fears within and between our sessions. He sent the applications in and was accepted. Once in the program, there were two instructors who saw his talent and took him under their wings. Michael soared!

Within a few months, he was showing his work in galleries. After about a year, he had a showing that was written up in a major newspaper, and a major magazine featured an article on his work. He won an award for his art, and by the end of the second year, he was invited to show his work in China. At that moment, the vision his soul revealed to him in my office started to manifest in reality.

Since that vision first appeared, Michael had and continues to have all the talent and ability he needs to accomplish whatever his soul has in store for him. There are challenges along the way. The work is intense. He learned how to take care of his body to build strength and energy. At the same time, the work is also his joy. Joy is the byproduct of actualizing the soul's purpose.

Even though he has no way to know what is going to happen next, he is beginning to trust that the resources he needs will be there for him. At each step in the journey, he meets people who, inspired by his vision, become part of a team that supports him. This is quite common when you have a clear purpose.

Michael is 20-something; he's a millennial. Once he took the first step, the next step quickly appeared. This all unfolded in a very short time. His ego did not spend 40 years reinforcing the original structure before he heard and began following his soul's call.

Usually by midlife it takes quite a while to identify and metabolize patterns that have long been ingrained in your view of yourself and your way of being in the world. The ego requires more time to trust the soul's leadership and renovate the old boundaries. This is not an easy road. Most people never even attempt it, which is why M. Scott Peck called it the "road less traveled."

I'm excited that this information can support more people and especially young people to heed the call of their souls early in life. My vision is that it can become the "road most traveled."

Love Smoothes the Way

You yourself, as much as anybody in the entire universe, deserve your love and affection.

—Buddha

Exploring the journey again through my clients' experiences and stepping back to view the seemingly disconnected mosaic of my own experiences helps me understand how the journey into an enlightened life unfolds through this loving ego-soul dance. Once the soul takes the lead in the dance, you experience more confidence, ease, and personal satisfaction in all areas.

The ego, the soul, the structure—it's all us! There is no point in hating or resisting any part of it. What's important to understand is that there is a process involved. When you know that, you can use the process to transform your life to confidently follow the call of your soul. This is your unique path. Just as the acorn inevitably becomes an oak tree, unless stopped, the seeds that created you inevitably unfold the unique person you are destined to be.

The ego is about serving the soul's needs. Early on, the soul needs protection, because experiences in the world teach the soul it needs to back up: *"Stop being so curious,"* *"Stop talking so much,"* or whatever the disciplines were. *"Sit down and read your book"*; that's one that I got. So when I was stressed, I isolated and tried to figure out what was going on to learn more about what was happening.

The soul reflects your true nature. The ego is trying to protect you from the impulses of that nature for which you got disciplined—the original consequences of being your natural self.

Early on, the ego's structured approach helps us to live in the world more successfully, more comfortably. Then, at some point, it becomes too confining. After all, the soul is destined to unfold just like a plant unfolds from its seed. It is not painful unless you put constraints on it.

Think of a tree sapling. You prop it up and put a support on it in the beginning, so it can grow straight. But if that support stays on too long, it cuts into the bark of the tree, injuring it and exposing it to damage and disease. You must remove the prop at some point so the tree can realize its full growth potential.

As the ego holds on, the soul is pressured. This is the dark night of the soul; it is the transformation point. Without it, we do not have enough pain, enough angst, and enough motivation to do something different. In the addiction field, it's called "hitting bottom."

How much pain we need to endure before seeking a way out varies from person to person. Fear keeps us stuck. Love moves us forward—love of life, and love of the truth of who we are and our purpose. Love and compassion for you and your journey move you through the ego fear of exploring the unknown.

Acknowledge the Fear

As you take steps forward, you can count on the ego to be afraid. Fear is part of the process. Acknowledging the fear is far better than ignoring, overriding, or trying to push through it. Of what exactly is the ego afraid?

Ego fear is what Marianne Williamson refers to in this well-known quote from *A Return to Love*: *"Our deepest fear is not that we are inadequate. Our deepest fear is that we are powerful beyond measure. It is our light, not our darkness, that most frightens us."*

The ego is afraid that if the soul experiences liberation, it will attract the same dire consequences as in the past. To discover what your ego might fear, you can ask paradoxical questions: *What's the downside of feeling powerful or having what you want?* or *What's the upside of not making a change and keeping the status quo?* Or, you can just take a step forward or imagine taking that step, and observe the thoughts and feelings that arise to stop you.

Angela is a client who felt her soul was calling her to go to a craft show. When she displayed her unique craft before, her partner always went along. One time her partner couldn't go with her. She was afraid to go alone, yet felt a deep desire to take the risk to grow her business and herself in the process by going anyway. Her mind immediately brought up obstacles (*not enough money, can't afford the time off*).

She felt so strongly that she needed to go that she pushed through the resistance and finally went to the craft show by herself. I received a text message from her at the show: *"So glad I came! Great to see everyone again and I even got a new order!"* She felt elated! Angela followed her soul's call, which reinforced her desire to expand. The story doesn't end there, though.

On the last day of the show, on her way back home, Angela felt sick. She thought it might be the flu or bronchitis. A physician gave her steroids. The medication didn't touch her symptoms. This is frequently a clue that the illness may be emotional rather than just physical. She was adamant: *"I know I'm very sick because I always get nightmares when I get sick like this, and I woke up with one the night I came home."*

"Tell me about the nightmare," I prompted.

"An old boyfriend implicates me in an evil crime. There is no way out of it. I'm feeling powerless. It's hopeless."

Here we see the ego threatening what will happen if she continues to be strong and independent. What happened right before this? She felt strength, determination, joy!

We explored the sensation of fear in Angela's body. It showed up as a pressure on her solar plexus. As she observed the pressure without judging it, she felt it was trying to bully her to back off her desire to expand the business. I had an intuition to ask, *"Is it a bully or a bodyguard?"*

Her eyes lit up as she exclaimed, *"A-ha—that's it! I get it!"*

Changing the perception of the ego from an evil bully to a protective bodyguard provided a key to how the ego was trying to serve her. At this point, Angela recalled a scene from childhood. She realized that her ego was trying to protect her from the deep disappointment and pain she experienced as a young child when she felt powerful.

Now, as an adult, she is very capable of handling disappointment. Once she recognized the old pattern, we used an acupressure tapping technique to release the painful childhood memory and update the ego. We also reinforced the wonderful feeling of accomplishment and reward Angela experienced when she took the risk to go to the show on her own. Her symptoms cleared up!

This process helps the ego consciously update the old structure to accommodate the wisdom of her soul's call to go to the show and her adult capability to handle the outcome of that experience.

The Value of Structure

> *We should conduct ourselves not as if we ought to live for the body, but as if we could not live without it.*
>
> —Seneca the Younger

You, like me, might wonder if the soul needs any structure at all. My original structure was to accommodate everyone else's structure in order to maintain relationships with them. Once that structure was gone, I felt adrift.

Remember: The ego structure also protects the needs of the human body that houses the soul. The soul experiences life through the body's physical senses. The body must obey certain laws of nature to survive and function optimally as a vehicle for the soul's experiences. At minimum the body needs just what all nature requires: air, water, nutrients, sun, movement, and rest.

Unstructured, I move through the day eating and drinking what feels good to me at the moment. I might go to bed at 2 a.m., even if I need to get up at 5 a.m. to get ready for an appointment the next day, and just go without sleep. If I don't want to exercise, I don't do it. I let go of all the externally motivated "shoulds" and just do what feels good at the moment. My soul didn't seem to have any problem with this whatsoever—for a while, until I had a wake-up call.

I can't remember which came first: constant bleeding from a grapefruit-sized fibroid tumor foreboding a hysterectomy or a mammogram that indicated a pre-cancerous crystalline structure requiring biopsy. It doesn't really matter. The important thing is that my ego was terrified into waking up. I needed to make some changes fast so my soul could continue to live in this body.

As a nurse, I made some logical connections immediately. These were female issues driven by estrogen. I was a big meat-eater who particularly loved beef, which is loaded with estrogen. Also, even though I represented and recommended supplements from a particular company, I wasn't taking their female balance supplement.

In an effort to avoid the hysterectomy, I immediately started taking that supplement and cut out the beef. The tumor started to shrink; in eight months, it was gone. The crystalline structure was removed in the biopsy, and I have never had another issue arise on a mammogram or thermogram since then. I learned my lesson.

Before I started therapy, I was like a gerbil on a wheel. Most of the people in my family tree died in their 40s or early 60s, so I figured I had to get all my living in early. In therapy, I realized there were three people who beat those odds and lived well into their 80s and 90s. The biggest factor they had in common was a zest for life. I made a conscious choice to adopt them as my role models.

I since discovered that having a great mental outlook and low stress is not enough. The older I get, the more vigilant my ego is about maintaining daily physical structures needed to protect my body and mind. The structure can adjust and change as needed, *and* there needs to be one to live in the physical world.

There is another observation that seems to fit in this discussion about structure or groundedness: When I weighed more than 300 pounds, I did not feel my weight. My focus at that time was completely mental and spiritual. I focused little if any attention or appreciation on the physical realm. I was married to an engineer, who primarily focused his attention in the tangible physical and emotional realms.

In my experience, people who are highly spiritually focused usually partner with someone who is quite grounded in the tangible physical world. I think this external loving relationship balance is a mirror for the inner ego-soul love relationship that seeks a functional balance to ground the soul's spirit in the tangible body.

The ego gives us roots; the soul gives us wings. We need a certain amount of groundedness in order to allow our soul to soar. Too rigid an ego structure tethers the soul and restricts its movement. Without enough structure, the soul may not survive long in the body or wander off on a lofty adventure without the means and maturity to actualize its purpose in the world.

The challenge of the ego-soul relationship is learning to successfully negotiate and renegotiate the balance between these dynamic partners. We'll explore how to do this next.

⚼

The following concepts summarize the nature of the ego-soul relationship:

- The ego loves the soul.
- Early in the ego-soul relationship, the ego's role is to protect the soul.
- The ego and soul form a structure of protection based on early experiences.
- Once the soul matures, it pushes against the structure of protection to signal the ego that it needs more space to fully unfold.
- The ego attempts to maintain the original structure as it fears consequences from the soul's movement based on early experience.
- Pressure from the soul pushing and ego resisting creates conflict and stress.
- In order to alleviate the stress, the ego must learn to trust the soul to lead.
- The ego learns to renovate the old structure through new experiences.

⋗ Practicing stepping into new experiences and registering their beneficial outcomes prompts the ego to shift its role from protecting to serving the soul's purpose.

⋗ The ego continues to provide a supportive structure to lovingly serve the soul.

Understand More About Your Ego-Soul Relationship

Before exploring the following questions, do the following:

➤ Set aside time and space without distractions.

➤ Call upon the non-judgmental perspective of your observer.

➤ Realize the answers are just giving you information from the past to serve your soul.

➤ Feel your heart open with love and compassion for all the experiences of your life.

Have you felt the call to do something different in your life's work, change a relationship, or create something new? What are the thoughts and feelings that arise when you seriously think about taking that new step forward? From what is your ego trying to protect you?

What answers do you get when you ask yourself: *What's the downside of feeling powerful or having what I want?* or *What's the upside of not making a change and keeping the status quo?*

Chapter 6

Transformation

What the caterpillar calls the end
the rest of the world calls a butterfly.

—Lao Tzu

Different Folks, Different Strokes

Everything, by an impulse of its own nature,
tends towards its perfection.

—Dante

Transformation does not refer to the kinds of minor changes we make in our lives every day. We might change our daily patterns, such as starting a diet or becoming a vegetarian, or changing a style of dress or a job. Although these behavioral changes can sometimes reflect that inner transformation occurred, just changing the behavior is not an example of transformation. Transformation is a 180-degree inner shift in a person's perception of self and relationship to the world, a complete shift in paradigm. Each shift brings us closer to the truth.

Some people experience spontaneous transformation. Buddha became enlightened sitting under the Bodhi tree. A near-death experience or other powerful shock can affect this kind of instant change as well. In telling Oprah about his transformative awakening from deep depression after sitting on a park bench for two years, Eckhart Tolle shared that he *"did not know how it happened."* Though as a result, he is now able to live consistently in the present and encourage others to do the same.

Early in my career, while attending an addiction conference, I felt called to learn how people make this 180-degree shift. That quest took me on a long journey of experiences that taught me how to do this. As a result, I am able to share with you and my clients what I learned about how to transform and also support you in taking those steps. The purpose of this chapter is to share some of that knowledge and experience with you.

Timing and Transforming

Our finest moments are most likely to occur when we are feeling deeply uncomfortable, unhappy, or unfulfilled. For it is only in such moments that we are likely to step out of our ruts and start searching for different ways or truer answers.

—M. Scott Peck

We are not ready to take on transforming the structure of the ego-soul relationship until we have a sense of stability and ability to manage life as a mature adult. Once you know how to take care of yourself effectively as an adult, you may feel the internal pressure to restructure the relationship between the ego and the soul.

You no longer need an over-protective ego and judgmental enforcer to keep you safely stuck in conformity. As you assume more conscious responsibility for keeping the body and soul safe and secure, it's time to encourage the ego to serve the soul's unfolding toward actualizing your unique purpose.

Not everyone chooses to engage in transformation. It is not part of every soul's agenda. Many, perhaps the majority, are satisfied living the status quo of social structures. They make the best of a bad situation and believe that rewards, if any, will come in the afterlife. They live by the adage "When life gives you lemons, make lemonade." I call this decorating the Well.

The Well refers to the feeling of being trapped in a narrow, deep, dark place with no apparent way out. This is the trapped feeling people recovering from addiction describe before entering the transformative recovery process. I learned this from subjects who participated in my research (*Phenomenological Study of the Lived Experience of Recovering from Addiction*). People who choose transformation feel a pull to find a way out of the despair of the Well. You and I are such seekers.

Conscious transformation is a process that includes stages of dissatisfaction to despair, a crisis or turning point, deconstructing the old paradigm or way of seeing oneself and the world, disorientation, reconstructing a new framework (ego structure), and living a new way.

These stages are not completely separate and can overlap. Also, there is no prescribed time spent in each stage or the process as a whole. It may move quickly in a few months or take many years, depending on the personal style and preference of the individual and the soul's purpose.

My process took a long time. I believe that is partly because I asked to understand the process and partly because my soul's purpose is to serve as a guide to others. My clients are able to move through this process much more quickly than I did. Also, having a guide that knows the terrain along with effective techniques makes the journey more efficient.

What I am referring to here is the first 180-degree transformation from the ego beliefs and patterns created in childhood to a truer, mature, less-distorted view of yourself and the world. This is not to imply that change only happens once. The first time, though, is the most terrifying and profound.

Despair Escalates

> *You don't go through a deep personal transformation without some kind of a dark night of the soul.*
>
> —Sam Keen

We can alleviate dissatisfaction and despair in many ways and for many years before arriving at a turning point. The old methods of distraction or temporary relief stop working. The old structure no longer serves us, and we decide there must be another way. Or, we attract someone who intervenes with a call for help.

I was talking to a friend about this when he said, *"I already went through my midlife crisis. I got the sports car, I divorced and started dating, and here I am again. I used to be able to compartmentalize my thoughts and feelings. I can't seem to do that anymore."* He thought he changed himself. What he changed were external behaviors. He was trying to relive youth in a new way. Recently diagnosed with a degenerative illness, he is now compelled to contemplate his life in a new way. This is an example of the old structure collapsing. Previous defense mechanisms developed by the ego in childhood just don't work anymore.

Illness, especially chronic, autoimmune, or life threatening illnesses, can be a critical wakeup call from the soul.

When I was in nursing school an instructor said, *"Eighty-five percent of all disease and illness is due to stress."* The minute she said this, a light bulb went off in my head. I wondered, *"If that's true, why aren't we helping people get rid of their stress so they don't have to be ill?"* This was a significant moment when my soul called me to my work in health promotion with a focus on helping people alleviate stress. When people change their perspective and stress levels, symptoms often disappear.

While helping others, I was also learning how to relieve my own lifelong angst. Focusing on helping others is a way to relieve your own discomfort by distracting attention from yourself to attend to the discomfort of others. It's called co-dependence. This defense mechanism stopped working abruptly one day.

Upon awaking, I felt completely fatigued. I sat on the sofa and pulled a comforter over my head. I didn't want to see anyone, talk to anyone, leave the house, or move, and I didn't have a clue what was happening or what to do about it. Prior to this moment, I was a great problem-solver and taught stress management for 25 years. For some reason, my mind went blank. I'm not sure how long I sat there before taking the cover off my head. When I did, suddenly a thought arose: *What if I died right now? Who would do all this stuff?*

On the heels of that thought, the future unfolded before me like a movie. I could see my family, friends, clients—everyone—carrying on just fine without me. In that moment, it became clear that the extraordinary amount of "stuff" I did was only serving to keep me busy enough to stay disconnected from my deep despair. I took on more and more until that defense finally collapsed.

I have a friend who took care of her husband for many years before he died, then brought her ailing mother to live with her and focused on taking care of her mother for many more years. After her mother died, she developed a number of health issues, which are not responding to any treatments Western medicine has to offer. This is a clue that the issue is not strictly physical. The soul is calling for a deeper solution. Even though we have been friends for many years, she just recently said, *"I need to do something different. Let's talk."*

When you seek the truth, your soul calls you to transform. It doesn't stop calling you; it raises the ante until you wake up. The original ego defenses no longer work and distress escalates to a crisis point. Then you feel forced to make a radical change. The crisis point could be anything.

Crisis: Night Terrors—A Turning Point

*And the day came when the risk it took to
remain tight in the bud was more painful than
the risk it took to blossom.*

—Anais Nin

As I started to grow spiritually, and change my beliefs
and perceptions of life in substantial ways, I began to
experience night terrors. About 15 minutes into sleep, I
had a sudden feeling of being killed by some entity beside
me. It did not have human features of any kind. I was
just about to die when I awoke sitting straight up in bed,
screaming at the top of my lungs.

Once I woke, it was easy for me to go back to sleep.
This was not a nightly occurrence; it was random. It even
happened on occasions when I was away at a hotel or
spending the night at another person's house. There was
no way to predict when the terror would come and nothing I could do to stop it.

I consulted a psychologist, psychiatrist, and counselor
friends. No one knew what this was or what to do about it.
One day a friend who was a gifted psychic offered to do a
reading for me. After the reading, I asked her if she knew
why I might be having night terrors.

She knew exactly what was going on. Here is what she
told me: *"Oh, that happens when you are moving forward*

on a spiritual path so fast that the ego thinks it is going to die. You have to reassure your ego that it is not going to die and that you still need it in a different way than you needed it before." As soon as she said that, I *knew* it was the truth.

She went on to tell me exactly what to do. *"Sit on the bed before you go to sleep and talk to your ego. Let it know you appreciate what it does for you and that now you want it to support your spiritual journey."* I did this for two nights and never had another night terror. Since I started sharing this story in presentations, often people come up at the end to share their relief at finally having some way to understand their night terror experiences.

The ego thinks that once we start living from the soul, it's going to die. We need to reassure it that is not our intention, and that we respect and value the service it provides. After all, we still have to pay our bills and live in the world. So we need to converse with the ego and help it understand. Ask for its cooperation and support.

This is another foundational experience for the premise of this book. The ego and the soul are partners in a lifelong journey of growth and change. One cannot be ignored in favor of the other. They've been working in tandem since day one. When we learn to respect, value, and work with this inner relationship, when we learn to observe our inner dynamics with non-judgment and when we have compassion and love for all the parts of ourselves, life becomes an amazing and rewarding experience.

Can we do this without a crisis point? That's a good question. I don't know. Perhaps, once you know these dynamics, you can effect transformative change without the significant pressure of a crisis point. In my experience, we don't make this kind of dramatic change without a compelling reason.

The old paradigm may not be pleasant, yet it is comfortable because it is familiar. The pain of staying in that comfort zone has to become greater than the risk of leaving it in order to transform.

Deconstructing the Old Paradigm

> *Re-examine all you have been told in school or church or any book and dismiss whatever insults your own soul.*
>
> —Walt Whitman

Our circumstances of birth and conditioning create the structure through which we see the world. Though we cannot change the circumstances, with the right support, we can change our view and with it the structure. This must happen before radically different choices are clear or possible.

Once the ego structure is in place, it stays in place until we either consciously change it or something radical happens that tears it down. I think of the original ego structure like an erector set, built of strong metal pieces held together by bolts that are rusted in place. Dismantling or renovating this kind of structure requires tools.

We struggle against ego fear in deconstructing these preconceived patterns. The more aware, compassionate, and open you can be to seeing and appreciating the old structure and its purpose, the less painful the dismantling process can be. This is where releasing the enforcer and having a strong, curious, non-judgmental observer are critical. It is also enormously helpful, if not essential, to have a teacher or guide to create a safe, non-judgmental space for exploration and to support persisting in the process.

We are all unique. Our egos are unique; our souls are unique. Despite this, the conditioning process is about conformity. You learn that there is a "right" and "good" way you "should" be. The worst part is there is a perpetual gap between the reality of your true nature and this ideal image of the person you think you should be. The conditioning process sets us on a mission to continuously strive to become the ideal image. I call this ideal image and the drive to achieve it "the perfection myth."

I realized this while working with healthcare professionals in addiction recovery. Even though the participants were successfully following their recovery program and maintaining abstinence from mood-altering substances, they continued to experience tremendous suffering. In capturing the essence of what they told me, a model formed in my mind for describing the problem as well as a solution.

The more I explored this paradigm, I saw that I also struggled with it. Sharing the model with thousands of people over the years, I now know it is a common human experience and the key barrier to living the soul's call. As a result, I developed a program to address it called "Breaking the Perfection Myth."

Briefly, we have an image in our minds of the ideal. That ideal relates to gender (*a good man or woman should*), roles (*a good wife, father, daughter, cousin should*), occupation (*a good nurse, engineer, entrepreneur, supervisor should*), body (*the right size, shape, color is*), and all manner of behaviors. These criteria come from early conditioning by parents and continuous updating by teachers, media, peers, religious leaders, and more.

All advertising is based on the premise that you need a particular product to be more "successful" according to some external measure. And that measure can change. The criteria for how women "should" look changed when I was in seventh or eighth grade. My friends and I all started dieting then. We weren't fat at all, but Twiggy was the model of the year. By that measure of success, we were *all* fat. I don't recall that there even was a dress size zero at that time.

The pharmaceutical industry creates new diagnoses from common human experiences, then advertises the medicine we need to get from our health practitioner to treat those "symptoms." In the early 1970s Valium became popularized as "mother's little helper" by the Rolling Stones. At a party once, I heard someone ask, *"Does anyone have a Valium?"* Nearly all the women in the room opened their purses. Who doesn't get a little nervous sometimes?

We are taught to strive to achieve the ideal. You have heard the classic advice "Practice makes perfect"—or its escalated version "Perfect practice makes perfect." This is an impossible task because you also know that nobody *is* perfect. Most of us are not consciously aware of this catch-22. When I point it out to people, they almost gasp at the obvious impossibility of this driving force in their lives.

As you put tremendous time and energy into achieving unachievable images, you have no alternative but to feel like a failure. The descriptors people use for how it feels to strive unsuccessfully through time also describe the feelings of living in the bottom of the Well: hopeless, exhausted, powerless, frustrated, angry, helpless.... The worst part is, because no one talks about this, we all think we are the only one who feels this way and that we have some intrinsic defect that keeps us from achieving our ideal.

This belief that at our core we are worthless and deficient creates a huge barrier to looking within. The fear is that if we look, we will uncover the full horror of how awful we really are. I believed this, too. Nothing could be further from the truth.

Along these lines, the perfection myth is supported by the concept of "original sin," that black splotch on the soul that is attributed to our "fall" as humans. We are encouraged to continuously work against this inevitable vice in our being, even though it can never be erased. It's also reinforced by the hierarchical letter grading system in school. If you get straight As and one B, what is the focus of attention? The result of grading on a curve is the foundation of this t-shirt truism: *The world is run by C students.*

As a commuter during my freshman year in college, I had to wait for my ride. He happened to be a senior psychology major. This was a convenient reason to become a participant in some of his research projects. I learned a valuable lesson about quantitative research when he decided not to use me after the first three experiments. He told me, *"You are always in the 3–5 percent on the ends of the curve that I have to throw out of the data."* I retorted, *"If it's not true for 6–10 percent of the subjects, then it's not true. You should be studying us!"*

Coffee, eggs, carrots, and a host of other things are either "good" or "bad" for you based on the research studies you choose to read. Interestingly, studies in quantum physics prove there is no strictly unbiased research, as the perspective of the researcher influences the results. Nevertheless, we persist in looking outside our own experience for the experts with the truth about how life works and what we "should" do to improve ourselves.

People who have inner strength, stamina, and endurance can strive for a lifetime. Many numb the pain of constantly failing to achieve their inner ideal through all types of addictions. The belief that "more is better and there is never enough" is the definition of addiction. Some people just give up striving. They don't feel better about themselves; they just finally see the futility in continuing to try.

We waste tremendous amounts of time, energy, and resources trying to achieve this myth. It sets us in competition with one another for who is more perfect, and provides the criteria for being judgmental of self and others. It destroys self-esteem, which is the source of most social problems. This belief pervades and degrades our lives with little permanent reward and no apparent way out.

The good news is there is a way out! Reconnect with your original true nature and construct a new belief system that can support the soul's unfolding. Breaking free of the perfection myth is the key to feeling less stressed and living the satisfying life to which your soul is calling you.

Love, happiness, and joy are your birthright. To access these qualities, you must deconstruct the old paradigm and build a new one. This is not as simple or effortless as it may sound. Have you ever renovated part of a house while you are living in it? Imagine ripping out your entire kitchen, then trying to do all the things the kitchen supported you to do without it. For starters, the experience is disorienting.

Disorientation

> *"Who are you?" said the Caterpillar.... "I— I hardly know, Sir, just at present," Alice replied rather shyly, "at least I know who I was when I got up this morning, but I think I must have been changed several times since then."*
>
> —Lewis Carroll,
> *Alice's Adventures in Wonderland*

Taking down the walls of the ego structure in which you lived for so long can be disorienting. Without the mask and the rules that hold up the old paradigm, you don't know who you are or what is true anymore.

This space between the old and the new can feel like a void, or you might feel shaky, foggy, disoriented, and/or confused. This is why schools of transformation since the beginning of time advise you to have a qualified teacher, who has been through the process, to guide you.

A teacher can provide a safe temporary structure to support you through the upheaval by continuously bringing you back to the present, to sense what is real and true. Taking down parts of the structure step-by-step can be manageable with a few new skills. There is a risk, though, that if you take down a key supporting wall, the entire structure can collapse all at once. Think about what it might feel like, in a disaster, where in a moment you suddenly lose your entire house and neighborhood.

I attended the Ridhwan School for many years. The *Diamond Heart Approach* has wonderful processes and teachers to explore structural renovation in a safe way. Even so, midway through each 10-day program, many people experience feeling wobbly. I recall my last powerful deconstructing experience in the program. They call it the Citadel.

At the end of the experience, I had a spontaneous nosebleed that wouldn't stop. We tried everything without success. Eventually, I was hemorrhaging so profusely that I had to go to the emergency room for treatment. The physician packed my nose and sent me back to the facility.

I felt wiped out, dizzy, and disoriented. I didn't even have the strength to sit up in a chair.

As I lay on the floor of my room, many friends in the group, all healers of various kinds, ministered to me. It was more than comforting. I am filled with gratitude as I remember how each one compassionately helped me re-orient to where I was and inspired confidence that I would get through the ordeal. I don't know how it would have been without them, and I am thankful I didn't have to find out.

Back home shortly after this experience, I was sitting at the computer on my 55th birthday realizing that everything in my life had changed. All my old roles were gone. I no longer resembled the person I had been before. My parents died, so I was no longer a daughter. My children married, so I was no longer a mother. My marriage ended, so I was no longer a wife. For the first time I was living alone with no one to account for except me. The questions arose: *Who am I? What is my purpose, now?*

While pondering these questions, I suddenly got an inspiration to change my last name. The name I took when I married no longer represented me. Going back to the name I was given at birth wasn't me, either. I was prompted to go online and put "meaning of names" in the search box. I began to explore.

During the process, I realized my first name was no longer suitable either. I finally settled on Aila Accad, which means "light-bearing vessel." It occurred to me that the current period of my life is about being a vessel for light in the world, inspiring others to turn up their light.

My soul called me to construct a new way to live beginning, with selecting a new name by which to identify myself. Interestingly, I don't feel attached to this name or identity. It's just a convenient way to identify myself in the world. When people call me by my old name, it doesn't bother me. One label is as good as another. Disorientation disappeared once I connected with the unchanging ground of being within my soul, that which abides through all the outer changes.

Creating New Structure

> *Personality can never develop unless the individual chooses his own way, consciously and with moral deliberation.*
>
> —Carl G. Jung

I used to say, *"My life is totally unstructured."* That was true to a point. I did not do anything in a predictable pattern. I didn't go to bed or get up at the same time. When I get up, I do whatever seems desirable first. It may be a shower, it may be to make coffee, or I may go through the mail or get on the computer. As I started to be more conscious of the value of the ego's role in my life, I realized that this randomness *is* my structure. In fact, I would say aloud and relish the idea, *"I have no structure!"* It was part of my identity. This is also why I have been in business for myself for more than 30 years.

Then, I noticed that I take my supplements every day consistently. I would not miss one day doing this. It might not be the same time each day, yet it is a habit. I wondered, *"Why is this behavior so consistent?"* It is the only consistent thing I do every single day.

As I pondered this question, it came to me. I decided at some point early in taking them that they make me feel energized and consciously noted that they provide the foundational nutrition that keeps my cells healthy and alive. I never skipped this behavior from that moment. I don't have to think about doing it; it's part of the ego structure. It is automatic!

Life, growth, the soul's unfolding—these are all unpredictable. Habitual thoughts, emotions, and behaviors make up a structure the ego uses to make unpredictability safe and manageable. As the soul unfolds, the ego must adapt and restructure to allow more space, movement, and flexibility.

Transformation challenges the original unconscious early childhood ego structure. We can now participate as conscious adults in choosing how to renovate that structure to serve the soul's purpose.

This involves a daily practice of observation, release, and choice. As you strengthen the observer, you become more aware of your patterns of thought, emotion, and behavior and the effects these have on your energy.

Curiosity and non-judgment are essential to feeling open enough to explore. Observation with compassionate understanding of how these patterns served you to feel safe as a child, along with the awareness that they are no longer serving your soul's movement going forward, helps to release these patterns. Then, you can try new structures that serve physical and psychological safety and your soul's purpose.

As the ego comes to trust the structure of this practice, it relaxes, knowing you are not ignoring its need for structure. If you are lax, the ego will wake you up again with physical discomfort, emotional triggers, or worrying thoughts. As you feel well and relaxed more often, these reactions grab your attention quickly.

Observation involves not only observing your thoughts, feelings, and behaviors, but also how these enhance or detract from your life force energy. The level of life force, vitality, and energy indicates whether you are aligned with your soul's purpose or not.

Take an action, then consciously notice how you feel. Ask these questions: *Does this give me more life force energy? Does it give me more strength?* Focus on any factor that you associate with being more alive. Become mindful of how the action feels in every part of your body and being.

Notice and register that feeling consciously. You can say it out loud, write it down, or tell someone else. Do whatever reinforces the experience as true for you. I just notice the feeling in detail and acknowledge that in my conscious mind. As I do these steps, after a while, the ego just starts to work with me and prompt me to do it. I don't think about it anymore; the decision is already made on a deeper level.

One day I noticed as I got up from sitting at the computer for a long time that my body felt achy and stiff. This happened a few days in a row before I acknowledged it as an ego "wakeup" call. A couple of things changed in my routine, and I needed to explore a new structure to accommodate that. The place where I previously exercised closed, and I received a request to write an online course on stress. While my mind was energized and engaged, the energy in my body was feeling stuck.

I tried setting a timer for an hour when I sat down at the computer, so I could remember to get up and move each hour. I observed that, although that was better, it wasn't enough. I found a new place to exercise. When I went, I noticed how much I liked the music and registered the feeling of vitality as I worked out consciously in my mind. I also noticed I was smiling through the experience. When I was done, I observed that I felt more flexible as I walked and got into the car. I made the decision to exercise every day and noticed that if I went in the morning, I was less likely to skip going. If I did skip, I felt like I let my body down. This is the ego reinforcing the new structure.

That said, if you sit at the computer, as I have also done, and say, *"I love just sitting playing solitaire"* and you reinforce that this is the life you want for a few days or weeks, your ego will support you in doing *that.* It's indiscriminate. It is a little like training a puppy. There is one caveat.

Once you are conscious, you cannot go back to being naïve. It works against your soul's purpose, which drains your energy and life force. I did this for a few days. It got harder to move. I felt lethargic and unmotivated to do anything I had to do, like answer e-mail or call people back. Suddenly a thought arose: *Am I getting ready to die?* That thought woke me up!

I was disconnected from my soul's sustaining energy and the ego woke me with the thought of death. Then, the idea came to put on my Latin rhythmic soul music and get moving again. My ego also knows what makes my soul dance.

Being aware of these subtle patterns and studying how my ego works are how I've come to understand that the ego's service is to create a unique structure to keep my body and soul alive. My soul likes randomness, adventure, change. To be overly structured would bore me to tears. Yet, a certain amount of structure is supportive to life in the body.

I can see how my ego works with my soul to evolve beliefs and structures that work for me. Knowing this, I am able to consciously appreciate and support this process. You can do this, too.

Restructuring is a common dilemma when doing spiritual work. Have you ever participated in a workshop or spent time in an environment that supports you to be yourself? You're relaxed and getting all these insights and wonderful experiences, and then the questions arise: *How do I go back home and hold on to this? How do I go back into the world and avoid falling back into the same old routine?* That's the challenge. We have to work consciously with the ego to create new patterns that support and sustain the soul as it unfolds.

Your soul's journey and my soul's journey are unique. We each have a unique purpose and a unique way of unfolding that purpose. We can't compare ourselves to someone else or have a measure to determine *Am I on the right track?* or *Am I doing what I should be doing?* There is no external measure for this. It is simply a matter of observing and trusting your own soul's energetic feedback.

Once you select new structures, you don't want to get stuck in those, either. If you have not changed your routines for a while, make a decision to change something. It doesn't have to be monumental. Change where you sit to eat your meals when you're at home, or pack your lunch for a week if you always go out to eat. Change just one thing and see how it feels. It may be better or not. At least you are not unconsciously stuck in the same routine, the same structure, you had before.

This is what I learned through my own transformation process. Through observation and inquiry in the safe presence of qualified guides, I explored the thoughts, feelings, and physical sensations that make up the original ego structure. I was able to be both aware of the structure and transform parts of it with consciousness and compassion. This renovated the structure piece by piece rather than destroying it all at once.

Knowing the ego is a valuable part of us and that the ego needs a structure to feel safe and secure, we can consciously support it in creating new structures that serve the soul's purpose.

Observing the Process in Real Time

You never change the existing reality by fighting it. Instead, create a new model that makes the old one obsolete.

—R. Buckminster Fuller

Right now I am noticing how the ego and soul co-created a structure for writing this book. My home office is adjacent to the kitchen. After sitting at the computer a few times with no clear way to begin, I saw that trying to write the book in my office wasn't working.

My soul called me to find a new location. The ego thought I just needed to find a writing structure. Here's what the ego sounds like: *"You need to get all your notes, journals, and stories together; see what the themes are; then organize it into chapters. Or, maybe you should go downstairs and look at all your books that might be relevant to this subject. Or, maybe you ought to meditate and then draw a mind map. I think I remember where all the journals are and all those notes from* Diamond Heart...." The mental chatter goes on and on until I am overwhelmed and immobilized.

Well, not exactly immobilized. I still set aside time every day to get started, which did keep me moving in the write (pun intended) direction. That's when a thought came to gather some friends together and discuss the concepts I wanted to write about, record the conversations, and use the transcripts to get started. I set up three weekly soirées on Saturday evenings, found my old digital recorder, bought some batteries, and hosted the sessions. I love my friends! They were eager to support me, and we had some fantastic conversations. And I still didn't know where to start.

In the meantime, one day I was having coffee downstairs at the local Unity Church after speaking Sunday morning and saw furniture they were releasing to interested people. Two weeks before, I had a momentary thought: *"I need to find an inexpensive desk for the loft."* Here, a small computer desk that would fit perfectly conveniently shows up. I claimed it and picked it up a few days later.

Somehow, through all this seemingly scattered process of getting ready to get ready to write the book, I felt completely confident. My soul *knew* the book would be written and would be done on time. This is the clear "will" of the soul. The soul knows what it wants, and the ego wants to create a structure around it.

The week before Thanksgiving, the first structural change was put in place. I have no TV, so I borrow movies from the library and watch a movie at night before going to bed. I've done this for a couple of years or more. That week I decided not to borrow another movie. *"Maybe this time could be used for writing,"* I thought. Instead of writing, I tied up many loose ends in my business which freed up time to write.

Two days ago, the Monday after returning from Thanksgiving weekend in New Jersey, I woke with an inspiration. I took the laptop to the loft, set up everything on the desk, and decided to come up here every morning and write something. Just start. The ego immediately came up with a plan: *"Write until you have to leave to go exercise at 11:30 because they close at 1:00, and you know you won't go if you wait until afternoon. Then, come back, have lunch and write again."* Now, I see that the fleeting thought to find a desk for the loft, which conveniently appeared in my path, was all part of the soul's plan.

The little librarian in my mind just pulled this memory from the file drawer. I was telling someone a few weeks ago that when I brought my husband to see the house before buying it (18 years ago when we were mediating our divorce), he said, *"This house is you. I can see you writing a book in the loft."* I see that the ego has been playing with the book-writing structure for a while now, as it prompted me to recall that moment.

Whereas the morning part of the plan worked effortlessly for the first two days, writing after lunch didn't. That said, I took the recorder with me each day, and recorded many thoughts and insights in the car. Each morning I start to write using notes from the previous day's recording.

The observer noticed that I awoke with a huge smile on my face this morning, eager to get up and get started. I didn't even stop to make coffee, just got my supplements and protein shake and immediately came up the wooden spiral staircase to the loft. This is the perfect soul-full place to write: large windows with only a view of trees surrounding the house, plus, being winter, it is also the warmest place.

I just realized that I have been writing for two hours nonstop on something I did not intend to write about this morning. My intention was to transcribe yesterday's recorded notes first. The ego creates the structure; I choose to implement the structure; the soul inspires the writing. A restructured relationship for writing this book is born!

I am noticing, now, that the ego is feeling proud and wants me to recognize its contribution to the process. The observer compassionately smiles; *"There's the ego."*

Spiritual gurus, motivational speakers, and change experts all say that to live from the soul you must address the ego. Generally that means battling the ego. Unfortunately, this works against a basic principle of nature, namely "what you resist, persists." The ego fights back and fights hard. Understand, it is fighting for your life based on its original understanding of the young soul's needs. Guess who wins that battle.

I have heard people say, *"Eating healthy is a daily battle. You just have to be determined and never quit."* This may work for people who are driven and competitive. It did not work for me. When I hear this dictate, my soul cringes. Even Freud averred, *"Willpower is not enough."* When you understand the ego, you can approach it and enlist its support more successfully.

When I think of transforming the ego structure, I think of a house. The original structure is like a little bungalow, a starter home for the soul. Once you become established in the world, that house starts to feel too small and cramped. You might spontaneously move into a whole new house in a new neighborhood, or you can renovate the original house by adding a sun room or dormer, or you can open the space by adding windows, doors, or skylights.

When you make major structural changes to a house, it is useful to consult with an expert architect or contractor. Doing it by yourself can become disorienting and overwhelming, especially if you inadvertently take down an essential supporting wall.

The ego is about staying alive, and that mission is attached to your physical and psychological security.

Consciously taking care of your body, by developing habits that increase energy and stamina, helps the ego relax.

To the extent that we are mature souls, we know that the body is the vehicle for the soul's experience. As we come to respect, honor, and value that, we are now on the side of the ego. The ego is capable of working cooperatively with us when we appreciate it and understand that its mission is to serve our body and soul.

You need to reinforce and register the rewarding feelings and sensations from a new experience a few times before the ego trusts the soul's maturity. As the ego learns that unlike the naïve soul, the mature soul's movement in the world produces positive outcomes, it is more willing to co-create new structures to support the soul's purpose.

In the next chapters, we'll explore more about how to hear, discriminate, and live from the call of the soul.

⌇

The following concepts summarize the ego-soul transformation process:

- Transformation is a 180-degree inner change process.

- Although it happens spontaneously on rare occasions, transformation usually takes time.

- Despair escalates to a point of crisis.

- Old defense mechanisms and ego structures stop working.

- Crisis demands a complete shift in the view of yourself and the world.

- Disorientation and confusion can happen in the transformation process.

- The original ego structure must transform to support the soul's purpose.

- A teacher is helpful and may be essential to guide you through transformation.

- A new structure forms through observing, releasing, and choosing.

To Understand More About the Value of Structure and How Your Soul and Ego Negotiate Change

Observe how certain habits or patterns of behavior affect the energy in your body.

Notice how certain foods affect your energy about a half hour after you eat.

Decide to change one small habit or pattern for a week.

With curiosity and non-judgment:

- Notice how your mind reacts.

- Observe the emotions, energy, and sensations in your body from the change.

Chapter 7

Hearing the Call

> *The sacred call is transformative. It is an invitation to our souls, a mysterious voice reverberating within, a tug on our hearts that can neither be ignored nor denied.... When such a call occurs and we hear it—really hear it—our shift to higher consciousness is assured.*
>
> —David A. Cooper

The Moment of Truth

> *The apple cannot be stuck back on the Tree of Knowledge; once we begin to see, we are doomed and challenged to seek the strength to see more, not less.*
>
> —Arthur Miller

As soon as the structure of marriage, work, or school is gone, it opens the door for the soul to say, *"Ah, let's get on with our purpose."*

Once you are conscious, you can't go back and be naïve again. It won't work. You must find a new way. That way is following the call of your soul.

One day, while having my nails done, my nail technician bugged me to sample a weight-loss product she found. I resisted, then took it to stop her nagging me. Long story short, it worked. I became a distributor to buy the product wholesale. Within a month everyone wanted what I was taking. I didn't want to sell the product, so I gave them the number to buy wholesale direct. I started getting increasing checks from the company and had no idea why.

During this time, my EAP business was going through major changes. Those ended when I engaged a mediator to dissolve the partnership. By that time, the supplement business replaced my income. Through this call of my soul into supplements, I had powerful experiences connecting the body and physical health to stress.

I started earning amazing money, took 12 trips around the world, and earned two Volvo convertibles. It was a fun and rewarding time in my life that just unfolded without a struggle. Then, after 12 years, the company changed the marketing plan and that period was over.

I thought, *What happened? Money is not flowing anymore, and I need to make money to pay my bills, to survive.* Money was never an issue for me until this point, and now nothing I did seemed to work. What changed? I started scrambling for a solution.

A thought arose: *Maybe I need to learn about marketing and sales.* I attended seminars and webinars, read books, and tried to implement some strategies on my own. Nothing worked. Then I hired a coach to see if personalizing the approaches would work. It didn't. I searched my mind to see if I had an unconscious program stopping me. That didn't make sense, because I never had difficulty with money before this.

I used every stress strategy in my toolbox to keep the ego's survival fear from taking over. Finally, I threw my hands up in despair, asked for divine guidance, let go, and began meditating. After a while, maybe a few days, my mind became calmer and more focused.

Then, during one morning meditation, a vision, a clear image of a circle of women in my living room, showed up. An inner dialogue began. I got the message to have a women's retreat. *How many women?* I wondered. The number 11 immediately came to me. *What would we talk about or do?* A very loose format came to me. Just do a guided meditation at the beginning, provide lunch, and let it unfold. I felt this spontaneous, clear information just flow to me. Even though I had no knowledge or plan for how to conduct a women's retreat in my home, I felt a sense of conviction and confidence that if I just took the first step to schedule it, everything would work out fine. It did! This is the call of the soul in action.

In working with many clients over the years, I have seen this process unfold over and over again. It convinces me that at some point in our lives, the old structure simply stops working. Angst, disorientation, and in some cases downright panic arises. At the very least, the person feels stuck and has no idea what to do next. This is the time to let go and purposely listen to the call of the soul.

How Do You Know It's the Soul's Call?

> *If he closes off every passageway and escape route it's because he wants to show you a secret way which no one knows.*
>
> —Rumi

After writing the previous story, I pondered, *What are the key elements of the call of the soul, and what is the most logical sequence by which to share them?* I rearranged all the puzzle pieces several ways and realized it wasn't working. I needed to stop, let go, and wait.

This morning I awoke with the box top for this puzzle. I have goose bumps and a sense of awe at seeing in hindsight how the ego and soul collaborate to unfold my soul's purpose in this moment as they have through my entire life. The feeling of joy, love, enthusiasm—*en thios*—is present in this moment.

You see, my ego thought that my life purpose was all about stress relief. I could follow that like a fine golden thread through the tapestry of my life so far. I spent the first part of my life learning the importance of mental and psychological health on stress, then many years in therapy learning the importance of emotions and stress, then in the supplement business learning the impact of physical health on stress.

I thought the culmination was to share how to get fast stress relief with others through workshops and writing the stress-busters book. Then, the call to write this book showed up, and it seemed to take me in a new direction.

Of course, that's the ego trying to find a framework and lay out a plan again. *Are we supposed to talk about spirituality now instead of stress?* it wondered. I've learned to smile every time my ego tries to see the future. The thought that came this morning, the brilliant wisdom of the soul, is that learning to follow the call of the soul is the *ultimate* stress-buster! When the soul calls the message is clear and direct, and you know it is the truth. There's no stress.

The quest I set out on at age 9 is and continues to be the call of my soul. That story has all the key elements of hearing the call in it. The soul also unfolds in every client session—not only my soul, but the client's soul, too. It unfolds in every presentation. Now I understand why I could never successfully use a script.

The awards I received in Toastmasters were for "Table Topics"—that's speaking extemporaneously on a topic a person gives you at that moment. Speaking for me is about expressing ideas from the ego-soul collaboration in the present moment. The soul is continuously unfolding in every area of life. Even the content and title of this book are not what I originally set out to write. It unfolded perfectly into *The Call of the Soul.*

When you stand too close to a tapestry or mosaic, you can't see the whole picture. You need to back up and look from a distance to see it. An even better metaphor is one of those illusion pictures where you have to relax your eyes and suddenly the hidden picture emerges from the pattern of dots. That's what happened this morning. The hidden picture emerged.

All life unfolds this way. The unique feature of human life is that we have an ego-soul partnership that seeks to understand and express the meaning and purpose in life. My intention in this chapter is to give you the clues to how to do that, the clues to hearing the call of your soul.

Intention

> *There is only one journey.*
> *Going inside yourself.*
>
> —Rainer Maria Rilke

I didn't realize at the time or until now, actually, the full power of the original life intention that was set with my passionate plea at 9 years old: *"Holy Spirit, either tell me why I'm here and what this is all about, or take me back!"* It was delivered from the heart with heightened emotion and clear intent. My life course is clearly a quest that continues to unfold the answer to those two questions.

Every day, every presentation, and every coaching session begin, with setting an intention from the heart. The mind only knows the past, so it can only project a desire based on known experience. The heart communicates the soul's desire to unfold. The ego repeats history; the soul charts new territory.

The heart is the center of the seven major chakras, or energy centers of the body—the three lower earth-based centers (1. survival at the base of the spine, 2. relationship/creation just below the naval, 3. power at the solar plexus) and the three higher centers (5. communication at the throat, 6. mental at the forehead third eye, 7. spirit at the crown of the head).

The heart is the place of integration between the physical and the spiritual. The message you get from the heart is generally clear and direct. It could be represented in an image, words, or a sense of knowing.

This is how I set an intention. Take some deep breaths. As you breathe in, feel your energy and consciousness coming into your body and centering in your heart. As you breathe out, feel all the tension and thoughts clear from your body and mind. Once you feel clear with your attention fully focused in your heart, ask your heart, *"What do you want or desire for this ____ (session, presentation, day, chapter)?"* Or you could ask, *"What's really important right now?"* You can ask anything that your intuition wants to ask. What's important is listening to your heart.

Do not consult your mind during this process. If you notice your attention going to your head, bring it back to your heart and wait. Be patient. Your heart will speak to you.

Don't second-guess or try to analyze what the message means. Just write it down. You may not know the meaning of the message until later.

When you practice this process, after a while you will find it becomes easier and faster due to conditioning. Conditioning is a powerful feature of the body and mind. It works now, just as it did when you were a child. When you consistently have an experience, the mind registers all the sensations in that moment. The next time any of those features arise, the entire memory of that experience reappears.

When you have an experience of breathing, centering in the heart, setting an intention, and getting a message from the heart, the sensory data from all those parts of the experience are cataloged as setting an intention in your mind. After you practice intention setting a few times, you just need to start and the experience can happen automatically. The same thing happens when you meditate in the same spot every day. After a while, just sitting in that place signals your body and mind that it's time to meditate—think Pavlov's dog.

This is also why comfort food is comforting to you. If you think back to the first time you had that food, the experience was comforting to you. Over time you embed the association of that food with comfort. So, when you feel discomfort, your little librarian in the mind automatically pulls out the thought of that food and you reach for it without really consciously thinking about it at all. You eat it and you feel better.

I remember when I went to my therapist weekly. I would think, *What am I going to talk about? Nothing came up this week.* Then, I walk in the door and the floodgates open like magic. I revealed things to him and to myself that I was never conscious of before. This is conditioning. It is a valuable feature of the ego mind that you can use consciously once you understand how it works.

Trying to access information for writing this book, I carry a small tape recorder with me as I drive to and from my exercise program, which is a very familiar route. My mind is disengaged, so ideas and insights come frequently and rapidly during these drives. An additional factor, which may contribute to the consistency of the creative thoughts, is that by just bringing the tape recorder along, I informally set an intention to receive insights.

By practicing intention regularly, you condition intention in your mind. Over time, you can live more and more of your daily life, automatically listening to your soul's guidance.

Focused Surrender

Always concentrate on how far you have come, rather than how far you have left to go. The difference in how easy it seems will amaze you.

—Heidi Johnson

You will notice in the story I told at the start of this chapter there was a period when the ego mind was searching and focusing on finding a solution to the problem before I finally let go—surrendered. When I was writing my thesis, I came across a term for this developed by George Leonard. It's called "focused surrender." This pattern of focusing on solving a problem for a period of time, and then letting go, creates a powerful force for integration. A solution arises at a new level of wholeness.

Einstein frequently worked for an intense period of time on a problem and then took a nap. He developed his theory of relativity during one of those naps. That's what happened to me last night when I was trying to fit all the pieces together for this chapter. I went to bed and awoke with an insight at a more holistic level of thought from where the mind was working the night before. I found the box top for the puzzle I was trying to put together.

It is not problematic to allow the mind to work on solving problems that arise in your life. That is the function of the mind. It is also helpful to know when to stop and surrender the problem to a higher level of consciousness.

When you are engaged in the soul's unfolding, you are in the moment, taking one step at a time. There is no targeted goal or external criteria by which to measure your progress. The ego, being more about structure, needs a frame of reference. Also, because the ego is about remembering the past, it is helpful to acknowledge how far you have come and what you are learning as you go along. The ego is less oppositional when it can see movement.

My clients frequently get frustrated in the transformation process, thinking there is so much more to learn, or so much further to go to get relief. I find it helpful to remind them of how they felt and what they said when we started.

After a few months working together, Fran, a therapist, questioned why she wasn't able to feel the happiness she wanted: *"How is it that I can tell my clients the same things you tell me, and yet I'm not able to do these things myself?"*

Fran's ego had a destination in mind called happiness and an ideal image of how that "should" look and feel. I asked Fran, *"Do you remember how you felt and the things you talked about when you came the first time?"* *"Oh, yes. I was miserable!"* she recalled. *"Let's look at what's happened since that time."*

She noted that she made the decision to quit a job that was no longer satisfying and start a new business doing something she loves. She feels more relaxed and accomplished. She is making about the same amount of money with less stress and more time to do the things she wants to do. As she talked, her voice became more animated, and she had a big smile on her face.

I asked her to check into her body and notice how she felt in that moment. *"I feel good. I feel relaxed,"* she said.

Fran was always very serious. I pointed out to her that she was smiling: *"I didn't see you smile at all for the first few months. And today you've been smiling the whole session."* At that point she beamed with recognition. *"I guess I'm happier than I was!"*

There is no goal with the soul; there is no end point toward which you are moving. The ego has to learn to trust this. It can be helpful to keep a journal as you move with the soul's call because it can look like a crooked road as your life unfolds day by day. When you look back over your notes, you can clearly see the amazing changes and insights you gained in the process. This helps the ego relax.

Sensing

> *Emotion is the moment when steel meets flint and a spark is struck forth, for emotion is the chief source of consciousness. There is no change from darkness to light or from inertia to movement without emotion.*
>
> —Carl G. Jung

The senses are the soul's playground. The soul loves and learns through sensory experience. When I think about this, I recall the scene from *City of Angels* where Nicolas Cage, playing an angel, wanted the ability to sense so desperately that he decided to fall to earth and become human just to do this!

Being mindful of what you are sensing when you hear sounds, taste food, smell fragrances, and so on, attunes you to your soul.

The soul communicates through the senses, emotion, and intuition. Learning to be attentive to the body's sensory clues and emotion attunes you to the intuition or knowing of the soul. We give the brain so much credence and tend to ignore the wisdom housed in the body. To hear the call of the soul, you must begin to listen in a new way. In Einstein's words, "The only real valuable thing is intuition."

HeartMath Institute researchers conduct studies on intuition. In 2004, they found that unconscious perception is seen in subtle changes in emotions and can be measured through physical changes in the body. They also validated that intuition is not stored in the memory or cognitive functions of the brain. Their theory is that sensory data held in the energy field around the body provides the information for intuition.

We are learning, and there will be more science to back this up as time goes on, that the mind is not housed in the brain. The mind encompasses information stored in every cell of the body, in the field of energy surrounding the body, and between people. Rupert Sheldrake developed the concept of morphogenic fields, Carl Jung talked about the universal unconscious, and I heard Deepak Chopra describe the information field we tap into when we calm our thoughts.

Quantum physicists discovered that when they take an electron pair, separate them, and effect a change in one, that change simultaneously shows up in its partner, even at large distances apart. This is called "non-local effect" and may account for such common experiences as thinking about someone and that person calls you.

You may also notice that you get insights and profound awareness when your mind is at rest with some routine activity. Taking a shower, driving familiar roads, and engaging in other essentially mindless activity opens the door for accessing information from a source other than the ego mind. This might be called the higher self, the divine, super-consciousness, the universal mind, or consciousness. Whatever and wherever this is, it is wisdom or creative new knowledge that is not grounded in our limited past experience. When you understand this, you can use this strategy effectively to listen to the soul.

I was working with a client once who experienced ritual abuse in her childhood. One day as she recalled the abuse, I actually saw red welts appear on her wrists where she had been tied. This is clearly a memory stored deep in the cells of her body.

When a message is from the ego, it generally comes from our head; it is based on past information and the emotion underlying the thought is fear. When the message is from the soul, it comes from the heart, emotions, and sensations in the body. There is a sense of knowing and a feeling of confidence in the truth of what you know.

Clarity and brilliance are two qualities of the soul. The soul holds the template for unfolding your future; it calls you to experiences you have never had before.

The soul calls you from day one. The baby has no fear of moving into the unknown. The baby is called to crawl, walk, talk. The ego has no concept of these events until you experience them. Once you have considerable experience behind you as an adult, the ego thinks it knows how life "should" be and resists new experiences.

If you suddenly have an inspired idea of something you want to do, have no idea how it can ever happen, are enthusiastic and excited about the possibility of it, and your mind is coming up with every reason why it will not and cannot happen, you can bet this is a call of the soul!

Observe Fear

What you are afraid to do is a clear indication of the next thing you need to do.

—Ralph Waldo Emerson

You need a strong observer when the ego fear arises around the call of the soul. Observe the fear so you don't get pulled down and immobilized in the undertow of it.

The ego fears taking a step into the unknown without a plan. It will bring up all the reasons the soul's call will not work and all the things that could go wrong, up to and including complete disaster. Try to remember that its intention is protection and that it bases the fear on old information from childhood.

This is the struggle many of my clients experience when they are awakened by a call of the soul. The ego cannot reconcile leaving a secure job with benefits for something they have never done before and have no idea how it can be successful. We are used to measuring success by the criteria of the world ego. The soul's call cannot be measured this way.

There is no way to anticipate the outcome of what you are being called to, except to trust that the unfolding of your soul is the perfect plan for you. It is the template for your life. Flowing with it is your only real assurance of getting what your heart genuinely wants. This takes some practice. Once you step into the new and it works out great, the ego can begin to trust (in other words, it will get conditioned to this new pattern).

There is no doubt the soul called me to write this book at this time. My ego didn't think I knew enough yet to write it, so I didn't sign up to talk with the available literary agent at the conference. Regardless, other people intervened to introduce me to the agent in spite of my belief that I did not have a book she would want. Here I am effortlessly writing that book and learning more than

I ever imagined in the process! I have no idea what will happen next, yet I do know with confidence in my heart that whatever comes next will unfold just as it is designed for me.

This approach is *totally* counter-culture. You can expect resistance not only from your own ego, which is culturally conditioned; you can expect it from everyone else who is scared to death to follow their soul's call. Here is the question to ask yourself: *Do those people have what you want?* Are they happy, healthy, at peace, loved and loving, fulfilled, and excited about what the next day has in store?

Get ready. Those people will begin to distance from you. And, take heart. Within a short time, you will be attracting new people into your life who are on the same wavelength with you. In between, you may feel alone for a short time. If your ego fears abandonment, just know it might get scared. Get into your observer, be compassionate, and observe that.

Be Still and Know

Stillness is the language God speaks;
everything else is a bad translation.

—Elkhart Tolle

It is easier to hear the call of the soul when your ego mind relaxes. The best way to calm your mind is to observe how it works, and use its natural tendencies to help it relax and support your soul's call.

When the ego mind is in fear, it ceaselessly struggles to find solutions. These solutions can only be based on the past. This is why your mind continues to go over the same ideas in circles, repeatedly, which gets you nowhere.

This is especially present when the mind has no answer, as in the case of a sudden death, suicide, trauma, or accident. The mind is at a complete loss to explain certain things, and will drive you batty trying. I heard Deepak Chopra say, *"The mind has 50,000 thoughts a day and they are all the same thoughts."*

Security is not measured by the external state of your bank account, or anything else for that matter. Your kids or a spouse are not necessarily going to take care of you in your old age. I have a client who was afraid to leave her emotionally abusive partner because she didn't want to be alone in her old age. *"What if I need someone to care for me?"*

I asked her, *"How do you know he will be there to take care of you if you have a debilitating illness or Alzheimer's?"* Her ego mind had no answer for this.

You see, for all the logic we attribute to the ego mind, when it is reacting from fear it is not particularly logical. It is conditioned! I know I am repeating myself, and it bears repeating because this is a key barrier to hearing and following your soul's call. The conditioned belief is that spouses and children "should" take care of their partners and parents out of love and commitment. *Should* is the operative word here. It is at the heart of ego conditioning.

Mother Teresa is a good example of this principle in action. She followed her soul's purpose to be a model of compassion in the world. She lived in poverty, yet had all the important things most of us seek (love, joy, deep connection) and was highly successful in the world by actualizing her purpose in a very simple way.

Calming the mind is essential to hearing and living your soul's purpose. To calm the mind, you must trust that you will have everything you need when you need it.

The key word is *trust*.

The soul did not stagnate or disappear through all the years you grew and matured. It is always present and at times you consciously experienced its presence. The ego may not register these experiences as the soul's presence. Making the unconscious more explicitly conscious is one way to help the ego evolve more trust in the soul's capacity and capabilities. It can help to remind the ego that you made it through difficult times or times of major change before.

I ask my clients, *"Do you ever remember a time when you felt this way before?"* They think and eventually say, *"Yes." "Did you have everything you needed to come through that situation?"* After thinking for a minute or so, again the answer is, *"Yes."*

In answering these questions, the ego reminds itself that this territory is familiar and that there is a past experience of safe, secure success to draw upon. This is an excellent way to recondition the mind for more calmness.

Also, the mind loves to answer questions. Arne Rantzen developed the practice of asking "creative questions." A creative question has a positive answer. For example: *Why will I be successful with this project?* With this kind of question, you set up the mind to scan the memory database for past experiences, which show the qualities you have that can contribute to success in this situation.

The mind has no preference; it will answer whatever question you ask. If you ask a negative question, which is what we are usually conditioned to ask, such as *What might go wrong if I try this?* You will get a litany of good reasons not to do it. Ask a question to which the little librarian in your head can find a positive answer.

This question in my stress-busters book is *What is right in this moment?* or *What am I grateful for right now?"* Ask that now and wait for the answer. I will predict that your mind came up with something. And, if you wait a few more moments, it will start to make a list of all the things that are right. Eventually, your heart will open with gratitude for all the wonderful things in your life.

Did you do the exercise I just suggested? If the answer is yes, keep reading. If the answer is no, I strongly urge you go back and do it. Just understanding this concept will not serve you. You must give your mind the actual *experience* in order for it to change. If your ego is resisting doing the exercise, observe that.

Being still also relates to not being wrapped up in getting more of something and being at peace with what you have. A client once said, *"I finally figured it out! Happiness is appreciating what you have rather than having what you want."* This speaks to the concept of gratitude. We are conditioned by the perfection myth that more is better and there is never enough. The mind is trained to incessantly focus on what is not right or what I don't have that I need. This is the gap between what is and the image of the ideal.

When I was going through the adjustment to insecurity and uncertainty about finances, I found one particular bible verse especially helpful to easing my ego mind: *"The birds of the air don't have to worry about what to eat; the lilies of the field don't have to worry about what to wear, how much more are you loved?"* Every time I remind my mind of this, it calms down. Find a true statement you believe that calms your fear and put it in places where you will see it regularly.

Hearing the soul is easier when you live in harmony with your nature and the natural order of life. All the things you do that enhance your life force relax the ego mind. The ego is about protecting the body and the life force within it. When you eat what energizes you, sleep, drink water, exercise—all of the things that attend to survival of the body and acknowledge yourself for it—the ego is reassured.

You may be wondering why I haven't mentioned meditation. First, we all know meditation has the ability to calm and focus the mind. I am a proponent of meditation, and I meditate. I've used many types of meditation.

The reason I didn't put it here is that it requires practice on a regular basis and the ego is likely to resist it. Also, I know people who have meditated for many years and never addressed their conditioning or unresolved emotional baggage. Once the few hours of residual meditative calmness wears off, they are still fearful, angry, and frustrated.

Meditation is a wonderful practice and I recommend it on an ongoing basis to support hearing your soul's call. That said, it is not enough by itself, in my experience, to restructure the ego.

Feeling in Control

> *Get rid of your fear of failure, your tensions about succeeding, you will be yourself. Relaxed. You wouldn't be driving with your brakes on. That's what would happen.*
>
> —Anthony De Mello

The ego mind is all about needing to feel in control to be safe and secure. I learned this after teaching stress management for 25 years and then finding myself on the sofa with a cover over my head in a stress crisis. All of the strategies I used to this point seemed to be working. I realized later they only worked because I was strong, capable, and competent enough to pull myself up by the bootstraps and keep on going. It was the *illusion* of control that worked for a long time. Once that stopped working, I needed to find a new strategy.

The only things you can control are inside of you. Nearly everything that stresses you comes under three basic categories: time, nature, and other people. Essentially, everything outside of you is outside of your control.

We can have some influence in outer conditions to the extent that we exercise control over what is within our power. We are only in control of our own mind, emotions, and choices. The more control you have over you, the more relaxed the ego can be and the clearer the soul's call can be heard. My friend and fellow entrepreneur Linda Arnold said it best: *"Things got a lot better when I resigned as CEO of the Universe."*

Anything that triggers you, positive or negative, has a reference point in your internal experiential library. This is, as Ram Dass would say, "grist for the mill." If you ask to be free, you get more experiences that bring these issues to the surface, so you can metabolize them. This is what inspires the caution to "be careful what you ask for."

You attract to you the exact experience you need to metabolize next. The triggers become more subtle, so it is sometimes hard to see on your own. It can help to have a mirror. This is where a good teacher is helpful.

The great news is that this process supports restructuring the ego, so the soul has more space to unfold. Respecting and valuing both the ego and soul allows for less stress and more openness and peace. This is also true because it takes much less effort to hold up the ego structure.

Both—And

If we can stay with the tension of opposites long enough—sustain it, be true to it—we can sometimes become vessels within which the divine opposites come together and give birth to a new reality.

—Marie-Louise von Franz

The ego judges, categorizes, and compartmentalizes; the soul is curious, non-judgmental, and open to all possibilities. To attune to the soul, begin to open to the concept of paradox. That is when two apparently opposite or different ideas exist together in the same context.

The more you can see life with all its variations coexisting, the more you attune to the language of the soul. Either-or is ego language; both-and is soul language.

I learned a while ago to eliminate the word "but" from my vocabulary. When you make a statement then add *but,* you negate everything you just said before that. *"I love my job, but I wish I made more money."* Did you register the beginning of that sentence by the time you got to the end? Do you get the impression this person actually loves the job or is disappointed in it?

Use *and* instead. *"I love my job and I wish I made more money."* As you read this statement, you can feel both parts coexist as true.

When I feel elated, excited, and extremely up, I can count on a down feeling somewhere on the other side of that up feeling. This is not just part of my personal pattern; I've observed this in my clients also. It seems to be a rebalancing process. The more I am present in the moment there is peace, contentment, and observation with less inclination for extreme ups and downs.

In addition to ups followed by downs, you may notice both excitement and fear at the same moment. When you feel abuzz, is it fear, anxiety, or excitement? Usually we look for one label so we can judge whether what we feel is "good" or "bad." Taking away the value judgments, we can experience that the feeling is simply complex.

When I signed the publisher's contract for this book, I sent this message to my agent:

> "I am either scared to death or extremely excited.... Always hard to tell, since both of these come in the same emotional package. As I wrote that, I can see now why this is true. The excitement is the soul side of the experience. The scared to death is the ego side. They exist in the same moment. We can identify with one or the other, or observe that they exist as one!"

I learned this concept of two emotions coming in the same moment in therapy. When I started in therapy my feelings were numb. One day, I felt anger and passion at the same time. Think about the color of anger and passion; both are red. I learned that it is impossible to feel passion when I suppress anger. Once the anger released, suddenly passion showed up! Passion is the soul side; anger is the fear-based ego side.

As soon as you feel the passion arise when you tap into your purpose, immediately observe the thoughts and feelings of resistance that come up just behind it. This resistance can be expected. The ego is afraid that when you step into your soul's purpose, there will be consequences, just as you experienced when you first explored new territory as a child. Write down all the thoughts and feelings that come up. Writing them down gets them out of your head onto the paper.

This happened when I had the inspiration to write *34 Instant Stress-Busters.* Immediately I thought, *There are so many books on stress, who would want to read mine? You don't know enough to write a book. What if you can't find anyone who wants to publish your book?* Yada, yada, yada.

Here are some enforcer statements my clients heard just after they shared their soul inspired visions:

"You don't deserve to have that."

"You don't have the money."

"It'll never work."

"How arrogant to think you could do that."

"People will be jealous of you."

"Who do you think you are?"

Your observer has the ability to hold the space for both excitement and resistance. As you practice openness to paradox, you will open the space for a soulful perspective and relationship with yourself.

Read the Signs

> *When you fall in a river, you're no longer a fisherman; you're a swimmer.*
>
> —Gene Hill

When you open the space for your soul to call you to its unfolding purpose, opportunities appear and barriers disappear effortlessly. The signs that you are on your purpose show up all around you. It's like living in a new world, a new culture, where everything supports your soul's unfolding.

William S. Burroughs framed it this way: *"In the magical universe there are no coincidences and there are no accidents. Nothing happens unless someone wills it to happen."* By virtue of your intention to live the call of your soul, what some might call magical, things begin to happen. Two concepts showing up frequently are serendipity and synchronicity.

Serendipity means a "happy accident" or "pleasant surprise"; something good or useful happens unexpectedly. When my friend Joyce invited me to the freelance writers' conference, I had no idea or conscious intention to write another book. I just wanted to hang out with my good friend and have fun. I am still amazed as I recall that serendipitous moment when I met a literary agent, talked with her for about three minutes at a break, and suddenly heard her say, *"I want that book. Send me a proposal!"*

Even though I did not purposely set the intention to write this book, I set an intention every day to hear and live the call of my soul. It is an open rather than specific intention.

I am still in awe every time serendipity happens, although now it happens all the time.

Whenever I leave my house, I set an intention to have a convenient parking place when I arrive where I am going. There is always a space. Often, someone is pulling out as I arrive. At one time, these were pleasant surprises; it happens so consistently now I expect it and am surprised when it isn't there.

Synchronicity is when two unrelated things seem to happen by chance and share some meaning together. Carl Jung told the story of listening to his patient describe a dream. In the dream, she was talking about a golden scarab beetle. While he was listening to her, something tapped on the window. He opened the window to find it was a beetle, much like the one his patient described.

It is common for me to learn or be given a bit of information, and within a few minutes to a day, someone asks me a question requiring that information.

One day, I was looking out on the yard from my office musing, *What I need is a gardener.* Two days later, a neighbor I just wave to in passing messaged me on Facebook: *"I see you have a tree down at the foot of your driveway. I can cut that up for you if you want."* His last name is Gardiner! When you are paying attention, you will see signs everywhere.

When you find yourself pushing, prodding, frustrated with issues in the way of actualizing your purpose, either the purpose you *think* you have is not the call of your soul, or there is a lesson to be learned before you can proceed, or you are in a waiting period before the timing is right to move forward. In all three cases, I suggest you let go and set an intention to be open to your soul's guidance. Clear your mind; don't go there looking for answers.

The other huge sign that you are aligned with the call of your soul is enthusiasm, energy, and light in the eyes and face. My friend Harry flew in for work recently and took the opportunity to visit me. I invited him to come to dinner. He said, *"I'm bringing everything. We can cook together. It will be fun!"*

"You're my guest," I protested. He was so determined and excited about it; I had no choice but to accept his plan.

Arriving after a long day conducting corporate training, Harry wasn't the least bit tired. When he started cooking, you could see him glow! The food, cooked with love, was delicious! I said, *"Have you ever thought about opening a restaurant or being a chef?"*

About a week later, I got a call from Harry. *"Wait until you hear my idea! I'm going to start teaching cooking classes at my house. It's perfect! I'm going to..."* At this point, he laid out a clear, concise, confident plan with all the enthusiasm of a genuine call of the soul. I know he and his classes will be a great success!

Once you hear the call, it is time to live the day to day unfolding of the call of your soul. That is what we will explore next.

※

The following concepts summarize hearing the call of the soul:

- The soul responds when you listen with intention.

- The soul communicates through sensation, emotion, and intuition.

- Focusing on solving a problem, then letting go, creates the conditions for more holistic awareness.

- Sensory mindfulness enhances the ability to hear the call of the soul.

- Expect and observe resistance and fear with awareness and compassion.

- Quiet the mind through reconditioning to hear the soul.

- The soul unfolds in the moment. Let go of planning or controlling the outcome.

- Hold the paradox that two apparent opposites can occupy the same space.

- Look for the signs of the call of the soul.

Practice Hearing Your Soul's Call

Practice setting your intention using the exercise in this chapter. Keep a journal of the messages you receive and the way you receive them.

Practice asking your mind positive questions such as *What is right in this moment?* or *What am I grateful for right now?* Record the results.

Set aside time to practice eating a meal mindfully sensing all of the colors, smells, flavors, and textures of the meal.

Chapter 8

Living the Call

> *To find our calling is to find the intersection between our own deep gladness and the world's deep hunger.*
>
> —Frederick Buechner

Your Call Is Unique

> *Nature never repeats herself and the possibilities of one human soul will never be found in another.*
>
> —Elizabeth Cady Stanton

Everyone's call is unique. There is no hierarchy and no competition. The call of a teacher is no less valuable than the call of a professional athlete. People learn their life lessons and contribute to the world through all occupations and experiences. Each is valid and valuable. Just because one earns more income than another is not a representation of that person's value. That is the illusion of the ego. Some people who have the least can be the most soulful.

I recall a moment when I was driving across a bridge into downtown Charleston. A homeless person with all of his belongings in a shopping cart crossed my path. My soul called me to be consciously compassionate and loving in response to this man. The awareness came to me that he is a very old soul who was born to awaken us to compassion.

We are like facets of a diamond. Each facet has unique qualities and also reflects the qualities of the diamond as a whole. All souls have aspects in common, and each soul has unique personal aspects. Your personal aspects contribute to your unique purpose and calling.

You Have Everything You Need

> *Each soul comes to earth with gifts. Each soul takes upon itself a particular task.... Whatever the task that your soul has agreed to, whatever its contract with the Universe, all of the experiences of your life serve to awaken within you the memory of that contract, and to prepare you to fulfill it.*
>
> —Gary Zukav

You have strengths, gifts, talents, affinities. These are your innate capabilities and the things that attract you. Your unique mission, purpose, or calling draws upon these strengths and abilities. In other words, you have within you everything you need to be successful at whatever your soul calls you to be or do.

How do you know what these abilities are? I've identified three areas where you can explore clues to your strengths, talents, and abilities. These are your history, energy, and feedback from others.

History refers to stories people tell about you from childhood. I shared a story earlier about how finding my way back to my grandmother's house reflects a good sense of direction. It may also indicate an ability to stay calm and problem solve in a crisis, which is also a theme in my life.

Stories can be negative or positive, depending upon the story-teller's perspective. Even if the story sounds negative, look for the strengths underlying the story. As a child, Tim took his toy cars and trucks apart to see how they work. He was labeled "destructive." The strength beneath that so called destructiveness was actually curiosity about how the vehicles work. Tim grew up to be a gifted automotive engineer. Everyone has valuable talents or gifts, even if your parents mislabeled yours.

My daughter has qualities of determination and persistence. As a young child, these qualities can appear as obstinacy and opposition. We always seemed to be on opposing sides. I had to adjust my perspective to see her tendencies as strengths. As it turns out, her determination and persistence served her well through tough times in school. She ultimately graduated from college as a social worker and now successfully helps teens who drop out of school. Her soul calls her to bring her strengths and skills to young people who need them.

If you are someone who loves to help others, chances are you have had struggles that test your abilities and strengths. In this way you have firsthand experience, knowledge, and compassion upon which to draw to be genuinely helpful to another person facing similar challenges. The term "wounded healer" refers to this common experience in the healing professions.

Energy refers to the feeling you get when you are doing what comes naturally to you. You feel energized, time flies, and you enjoy doing it. This is the kind of feeling people have on the job when they say, *"I can't believe I get paid for this!"*

Feedback refers to the messages you receive from others who observe and appreciate your talents and abilities. Sometimes we discount this feedback as *"Oh, you're just being nice."* There are many reasons we might not want to take in that praise. From our conditioning we might have heard statements like *"You're not better than anyone else," "Don't go getting a big head," "People will be jealous,"* and *"Who do you think you are?"*

As human beings we are *both* unique *and* equal. When you claim and own your unique contribution to the world, it is easy and effortless to recognize the contributions of others. Giving and receiving accurate feedback is one of the best gifts we can offer one another.

There is a story I like to tell about my younger sister, Joan, that illustrates these principles. When we were children—she was about 3 and I was 6—we would go trick or treating at Halloween. She would bring her candy home and sort it into piles according to type: candy bars, pennies, lollypops, gum. Then, she would put it all back in the bag, pour it out and sort it again according to color: red things, blue things, yellow things, and so on. She'd put it all back in the bag and sort it according to size: large items, medium-sized items, and small items. She would happily do this for days. Joan has a natural talent and affinity (attraction) for organizing.

We were both distributors in the supplement business. The company faxed all kinds of information. I'd read the faxes and throw most of them away. Joan, on the other hand, organized them into binders. Thank goodness she is organized! When we needed to refer back to a fax, she knew exactly where to find it. She also uses this ability along with a talent for laying out information step by step to teach others. She loves to do this and she is good at it.

Joan consistently gets rave reviews from other instructors and her students for the excellent teaching manuals she creates. This is why I asked her to help me design the step-by-step guide for *Breaking the Perfection Myth*. She took my information and created an excellent manual.

My sister demonstrated a natural ability as a child; we can follow that theme through the talents she demonstrates as an adult. She has energy and enthusiasm for her work, and others recognize and compliment her talents. Joan has additional talents and abilities that are complementary to these. One is an artistic sense. Others may be organized, yet no one will have the unique combination that represents Joan's soul.

To live your soul's call, you must switch your focus from external measures of success to internal measures of satisfaction. Instead of focusing on the gap between who you think you are and the ideal you think you "should" be from the paradigm of the perfection myth, focus on actualizing your unique inner qualities and capabilities. In other words, shift the focus from striving for what's not possible to valuing what is true for you.

Once you identify your talents, look at the skills you learned that make the most of your talents. Talents come in your original package at birth. You learn skills from others. You become proficient by using those talents and skills through experience. Experience can occur anywhere, at home, work, volunteer, or church activities—anywhere you go you bring your talents and skills with you. You can't leave home without them.

Once you live from your soul, you get a sense of security from knowing the abiding truth of who you are rather than trying to live up to changing expectations set by others. This is your gauge for saying "yes" or "no" to requests and demands people make on your time.

Through time, as you follow the thread of your call you can connect with its purpose. Joan identified how her talents connect with her soul's purpose in this way: *"My soul call is to empower people to believe in themselves. I write the way I do to be sure people understand step by step how to move forward without me."*

No matter what your soul calls you to do, you have everything you need or will be given all the tools and support to accomplish that mission. There is an adage that has stood the test of time: "God doesn't give you anything without the ability to handle it."

Living With Uncertainty

Take the first step in faith. You don't have to see the whole staircase, just take the first step.

—Martin Luther King, Jr.

The soul unfolds into the unknown. As the ego has more experience with the soul's process, it becomes more familiar and trusts the process a little more. The first few times is scary!

My favorite metaphor for this feeling is a scene from *Indiana Jones and the Last Crusade*. There was an intense moment when Indy is being chased by what seems like hundreds of guys wielding swords. He comes to the edge of a cliff. Across the abyss is a cave that holds his deepest desire, the Holy Grail.

With death imminent and hope on the other side of the abyss, Indy's only alternative is to step out in faith off the cliff. As he takes the first tentative step, amazingly the ground meets his foot. This happens with each step he is willing to take. Ultimately, walking gingerly over the unseen bridge, Indiana Jones walks easily into the cave, where he discovers the Holy Grail.

This is exactly how the experience can feel, like stepping out over an abyss with no ground under your feet. Yet, when you continue one step at a time, you learn solid ground is there and you uncover the most extraordinary treasures you could ever imagine. It takes courage, diligence, and trust—trust in the process, trust in your desire for the truth. Ultimately, you find more trust in yourself.

I have lived from the soul so long now that the power of the soul is no longer as frightening to the ego as it was at first. Fear lessens as the ego comes to trust the soul's process. There is always some fear because we are stepping into new territory, doing something for which the ego has no frame of reference. When you focus on the energy that drives your mission, rather than the fear, the enthusiasm of your purpose powers you through the fear.

As I write this book from trusting the soul, I am more invigorated and eager to continue than afraid of what will be revealed. In order to do this, I had to abandon the ego's strategies of how to write the book, set up an environment to support the soul's flow, and step into that unknown territory each day. I have never been happier!

In the beginning, the ego was afraid that I would not have enough content for the 50,000 words I contracted to give the publisher. Yet, one or two notes dictated on the tape recorder consistently expand to 2,500 words or more as I write about that concept. Yesterday, I calculated the word count so far. It seems to be right on target. Yes! That's the ego; it likes to measure progress. When you move with the soul, everything works out just fine. The ego is never sure it will.

The more you observe the ego and practice restructuring techniques, the more the ego can support the soul's unfolding. The ego can learn to shift more easily as you practice. It learns that change can be safe, especially if the change supports survival of the body as well as the soul.

Dieting to look better did not last. Exercising because I "should" did not last. Eating whole, organic, and lighter, because it increases my health, aliveness, and energy, and exercising because I feel stronger and more mobile works long term. When I get lazy about it or go off course, it is my ego that nags me to get back to it. Amazing!

The soul does not "should" on us. It just moves in unpredictable and unpatterned ways. One day a choice can be right for you; another day it is not the choice to make. The soul does not have rules for you follow. It's all about reading your senses and intuition in the moment.

Today, I stopped by a café to get a Reuben sandwich, which isn't exactly the healthiest choice in the world according to nutritional authorities. I don't get it often. The last time I stopped at this restaurant to get one, I parked the car in front and immediately got the feeling *I don't really want it.* Today, there is a part of my soul that attracted me to get one and it was incredibly delicious. When I was done, I felt great and still do!

When I think about eating this sandwich out of ego habit and check into how I feel, I do not want it. At other times when I am prompted to get it, it is exactly the right thing. When that happens, I feel no guilt, shame, or second thoughts. I just feel energized.

The ego and the soul speak to you in different ways. When you learn their languages it's easy to make confident choices freely in the moment without rigid rules and judgments.

Success Is Assured

> *Honor your calling. Everybody has one. Trust your heart and success will come to you.*
>
> —Oprah

One day I had an inspiration (call of the soul) to put all the stress articles I wrote and submitted online into a book. That book, *34 Instant Stress-Busters,* was conceived in February, self-published by May, and became an Amazon Best Seller in July 2009. It launched a new wave of seminar and workshop presentations where I sold thousands of back-of-the-room copies.

I didn't know anything about how to do this until the soul called me to this project in February. Once I took the first step, which was gathering together the articles, the next step showed up along with the means to accomplish it. When you are on your soul's mission it's like the skids are greased.

Once I had the book written, I wasn't sure what to do next. I went to a regular Wednesday luncheon at a friend's house, where she had about 15 people gathered around the table. When I mentioned the book, one of the women said, *"Do you need editing? I'd love to edit that for you."* She was retired and just loved editing.

Not only did she edit the book, she gave me the next step: *"You'll want to get a graphic designer to do the cover and layout the text for the printer."* As it turns out, she just retired from the highway department, where she wrote and published a book.

My friend Ron is a graphic designer. He designed the cover and laid out the text as a favor to me. I Googled how to copyright and get an ISBN number and found a local printer, and, before I knew it, I had a book.

Then, synchronicity happened. The day after I picked up the books from the printer, I received an e-mail about a teleclass on "How to Make Your Book an Amazon Best Seller." I couldn't believe it! I took the class and followed every instruction to the letter. Sure enough, the book became an Amazon Best Seller.

I don't want to give you the impression that this didn't involve considerable effort. It did. And, for the most part, the process went smoothly. There was one glitch.

The date set for the book launch was a Tuesday. The printer was supposed to have the books mailed to Amazon the Thursday before. I called Thursday to be sure the books were in the mail. They were not mailed and by all indications would not be until Monday. I had a moment of panic: *What happens if all these people order books and the books aren't there?*

My mind was jumping from one disastrous scenario to another. As the stress started to escalate, I noticed it, stopped, took a deep breath, did some EFT tapping, and asked a positive question. The answer was *Call Amazon and find out what happens.* I did and they told me how to handle the situation. I sign up as the merchant and send the books out myself. Simple!

I called the printer back on Friday to tell them not to worry. They said, *"The books were mailed this afternoon. We brought in extra help and got it done."* There was the miracle in the whole experience for me. You see, everything works out fine.

Why did I have to go through that glitch at all? I wondered. The answer is that handling that dilemma helped me get even clearer on my techniques and how I use them. As a result, my confidence in the book became stronger, and I was able to use the printer story as an example on a teleseminar the very next week! Living from the soul's call is not necessarily challenge free, yet it is always purposeful.

To the ego, the call of the soul is Mission: Impossible. It has no idea how to do it or how it will happen. Nelson Mandela captured this accurately when he said, *"It always seems impossible until it's done."*

Amy Tan in *The Kitchen God's Wife* sums up the risk and success from stepping into the soul's call: *"How can you say luck and chance are the same thing? Chance is the first step you take, luck is what comes afterwards."*

Your Life Purpose

*You are not here merely to make a living.
You are here in order to enable the world to
live more amply, with greater vision, with a
finer spirit of hope and achievement. You are
here to enrich the world, and you impoverish
yourself if you forget that errand.*

—Woodrow Wilson

Purpose is a force that energizes. It inspires you to get up in the morning. Your deepest values and purpose are not in your head but in your heart. To what does your heart respond? What touches you? What energizes you or inspires you? When you follow your true path or calling, you are invigorated rather than stressed.

I'm reminded of a story about a man who purchased a quarry. He didn't know anything about the quarry business. So, on the first day the new owner decided to learn about the work done there. He asked an industrious worker what he was doing. The worker replied, *"I am making bricks. They must be exactly the right size, so I use a special mold to shape them with precision."* The owner then asked a second worker who was also busy making bricks, *"What is it that you do here?"* The worker said, *"I make a living. By working here I put food on the table and support my growing family."* When the owner proceeded to ask the third worker the same question, the worker smiled broadly. *"I am building a cathedral!"* he said with enthusiasm.

Are you stressed by feeling stuck in a job situation that does not allow expression of your true talents and abilities? Are you working in an area you hate because you have been there so long it is hard to leave, or you need the money? This is a huge cause for work stress.

I have good news for you. You don't have to leave your job to improve your condition. You can do this from the inside. It doesn't mean you may not be called to leave, just that you can start with a spark of passion to energize whatever plan your soul has for you. Doing something valuable and purposeful can change your outlook.

Define your job by its larger benefit to the world. I was talking to a person who recently put in a phone jack for my computer. I asked him, *"How do you like your work?"* He said with little energy, *"It's a job."* This was a routine task for him, nothing exciting about it.

Then, I said, *"I am very glad you do your job, because for me you are facilitating worldwide communication."* He looked up with a big smile on his face. He could see the mundane task or he could see the valuable purpose it serves.

I shared this principle at a recent women's business meeting. I asked the participants to think about the purpose of their work. After the meeting, one woman shared, *"I really expedite interoffice communication and that enhances the relationships in the entire organization."* This woman previously saw herself as "just an administrative secretary." Once she expanded her view of the outcome of her work, she could see how what she did routinely made a significant difference in the overall quality of work life for everyone in the company. She immediately started to feel excited about her contribution!

Passion and Energy

Follow your bliss.

—Joseph Campbell

Passion is the driving force for following the call of the soul. It's a power greater than ego fear and tends to override it. You might have doubts, yet you keep going because you must. There is also confidence and joy when you tap into your soul's purpose. You *know* it is yours to do and you cannot resist it. Helen Keller describes this energy: *"One can never consent to creep when one feels an impulse to soar."*

The soul picks up sensory information from the energy field around your body. That field is also around everyone else's body. George Leonard wrote about a principle of nature called "entrainment." This is a feature of how we share energy. He studied this by placing pendulum clocks in a room. Initially the pendulums swung differently, and within a day or two, the pendulums synchronized. They swung in the same direction together.

We attune to the patterns of the seasons and tides. We also entrain to the energies of other people. Here's an example. You might be having a great day, then you walk into a meeting where everyone is arguing and griping. How do you feel after about 15 minutes? Frustrated, angry, ready to pounce? Then, there are energy vampires, who drain the energy right out of you. You feel exhausted after talking with them for a few minutes.

On the flip side, when you are in the enthusiasm of your passion, other people can entrain to that energy, too. This is what Marianne Williamson refers to when she wrote: *"Our presence automatically liberates others."*

Passion is a powerful energy frequency. It influences the energy around it. This is part of why, when you are on your soul's purpose, situations and people support your mission. Life has more ease and fewer obstacles.

This is the importance of entrainment. When you feel your energy being influenced by others, you can tap back into your purpose, and the passion comes right back.

It's All Good

*Everything, by an impulse of its own nature,
tends towards its perfection.*

—Dante

What you are drawn to may not look like a "soulful" activity from the ego's perspective. You cannot always tell immediately what the purpose behind an action might be. It is with hindsight that things often become clear.

One day recently, I was attracted to playing solitaire online. Then, I started playing it more often. I consciously wondered if I was getting habituated or addicted as I was playing one day. I realized that as I played, I was not vegging out, escaping, or distracting myself from something else that needed my attention. I could easily get up and do something else. Yet, I could also play happily for several hours. This made no sense to me; there did not seem to be any particular purpose served by playing.

As I got out of the shower one day, I wondered how the ego and the soul are reflected in the act of playing solitaire. When I am doing it, I am fully aware and alert to what I am doing. My observer is awake. There is no set time to when I play. It is random in that it isn't a habitual pattern. I have lots of energy. It has elements that are interesting and that pique my curiosity in the card patterns that arise. There is no judgment or criticism in my mind. My ego is perplexed and can't figure out what this is about. This experience has all the elements of a typical call of the soul without any productive purpose.

This week, I explored these thoughts with my personal coach. She asked me a number of questions and then said, *"Maybe your soul just wants to play. Does everything you do have to have to be productive?"* The minute she said that, I *knew* it rang true. I'm sure you can relate to the experience of knowing the truth as soon as you hear it. It is a soul message when it strikes you like a laser of truth right to the heart or solar plexus.

The elements of the soul are with us from birth. Think about a baby. Learning, play, curiosity, creativity, and moving with the moment into the unknown are all part of our nature from the beginning. Perhaps this is what Jesus meant when He said, *"Be as little children."* He may be advising us to reconnect with the true nature of our soul now as mature adults.

So here is a feature of living from the soul. It is always new and often surprising. You are not repeating history as with the ego's structured approach. Living from the soul is never boring, tedious, or routine.

Practice Moving With the Moment

To love oneself is the beginning of a life-long romance.

—Oscar Wilde

I often guide my clients in a practice for connecting with the soul. Set a time, start small (like an hour), and work up to half a day or a whole day where you have no agenda and no distractions. You might have to go somewhere less familiar to do this. Tune in to your soul's desire for what to observe or do moment by moment.

The first time I gave myself permission to just move with what called me was when our family changed our Christmas tradition. We reserved a cabin at a state park for a week. We packed up the gifts, some lights, and the kids, and bought a tree and food in the local rural community when we arrived.

My husband had an office party to attend back in town on Christmas Eve, and the kids wanted to make holiday visits to their friends. So, the three of them left the night before. I awoke in the cabin, in the middle of the forest, alone, with nowhere to go (they took the car) and nothing particular to do all day.

At first, I wasn't sure what to *do* with myself. After making some coffee and a fire, I sat in meditation and connected with what I wanted. Within a few minutes, I found a new approach to living the day by moving with my soul's promptings moment by moment. These turned out to be some of the most rewarding and memorable days of my life.

I was fully present: walking mindfully in the woods, writing poems, dancing in front of the fire, gathering pine cones, berries, and branches from the ground, and decorating the cabin with them. I can't begin to list all the mystical and profound experiences I enjoyed. I even made some life-changing decisions.

One morning, after coloring my hair since college, I looked in the mirror and decided not to color my hair anymore. Just like that. No thinking about it; no worrying about what others would think or how they would react. My soul spoke, and that was that. I laughed out loud, delighted with this sudden choice arising from seemingly nowhere! I had no idea what my hair actually looked like underneath and didn't care. As it turns out, I have my maternal grandfather's gene for pure white hair. I never went back to coloring again.

Living from the soul is delightfully effortless once you come to trust its innate wisdom. That may take some practice experimenting and observing the results. Once you do, you will not want to go back to living strictly from the ego's limited structure.

Soulful Living

> *Magic is believing in yourself. If you can do that, you can make anything happen.*
>
> —Johann von Wolfgang Goethe

Living from the soul is much less stressful as everything happens in perfect timing.

It is holiday time as I write this, and people are getting stressed because of impositions on the soul from expectations and old ego structures. I am amazed that when I am present in the moment, I know exactly what to do next and everything seems to get done effortlessly. There are also things that I discover never need to be done. I just thought they did, because we always did them that way before.

I was coming down from writing in the loft this morning and thinking, *I will go to the dentist, then come back and do more writing, because I should get more done today.* Here is the ego setting a plan and telling me what I "should" do. Before I got to the bottom of the stairs, I realized that on the way back from the dentist might be the perfect time to get a few gifts, as I would pass the stores I need.

Also, I am aware that my biorhythms are not the same in the afternoon. So, it makes more sense to use the afternoon for routine holiday activities. I am not sure exactly how the afternoon will unfold. What I do know is that I have options and tasks that can be accomplished in their right order and timing based upon the soul's prompting.

This day will unfold in exactly the most efficient, effective, and least stressful way. I can see both intention and trust in this statement. Trust allows me to let go of control and move with the moment. I know that what needs to be done will be done in its perfect order.

Moving with the moment allows you to be present with your life. It is not a matter of forcing or reminding yourself to be present. It is living in presence, which is so much easier and richer. As you register these experiences with gratitude, the ego relaxes more and more. This expands your ability to continue to follow the soul's unfolding wisdom more and more effortlessly.

Soulful Relationships

> *The beginning of love is to let those we love be perfectly themselves, and not to twist them to fit our own image. Otherwise, we love only the reflection of ourselves we find in them.*
>
> —Thomas Merton

You don't have to practice non-judgment or loving your neighbor or telling the truth and being authentic.

Once you feel unconditional love yourself, stop judging yourself, and appreciate your unique talents and abilities, you automatically start to look for the talents and abilities of others and appreciate their uniqueness. Diversity is not a problem, because you know on a deep level every one of us is valuable and unique. Life becomes simpler with less stress and more ease.

Your relationship with everyone else is dependent entirely on your relationship with yourself. I remember growing up that I didn't want to be anything like my mother. In my mind, she was overbearing and didn't have any power. My father seemed more spiritual and had the masculine power of being a partner in an engineering firm. He knew how to move successfully in the world.

It wasn't until I did a presentation for the Homemakers of America's Mother's Day celebration that I evolved compassion for my mother and myself as a woman. In preparing for that presentation, I researched the history of my mother's generation.

I came to realize her dilemma in having to leave a job post–WWII in which she was happy and fulfilled to allow a man to earn a living. I think my mom, like many Boomer moms, stuffed their anger. They coped and kept on going. I could see how she lost her soul power and continued to maintain control through the ego, through controlling the household. My mother had marvelous intellect, talents, and abilities, and the culture at that time left her feeling relatively powerless.

Reconnecting with my mother, women, and my womanhood was an important part of reclaiming the relationship with me. I had to process the covert feminine anger I learned and come to a place of reconciliation with women and balance in myself.

When you have issues in your relationships, the place to reconcile the differences is within your own ego conditioning. Once you do that, once you achieve peace within your own skin, your soul can be open to relating with others from a place of connection, depth, and authenticity.

The Soul's Legacy

We keep passing unseen through little moments of o ther people's lives.

—Robert M. Pirsig

This is a letter I wrote in deep appreciation for my brother's journey and his response to me.

> You have no idea the people you have touched through yourself and your gifts.... You just have to trust that you are doing what is yours to do and the ripples of that purpose serve the greater good of all of humanity.
>
> I don't know if you were aware of this when we were at Dad's viewing.... A huge number of people showed up from the newspaper notice. I was amazed

by the number of people who came that we did not know. The place was packed with people!

One man came up and told me the important impact Dad had on his life and early career (30 years ago). He wanted to acknowledge that and honor him by coming and telling us the difference his life made for others.

Congratulations! I am so glad you made the tough decision to listen and follow the Call of your Soul.

Love & :)))

Aila

᙮

Thank you Aila...this meant a lot! And I'm saving it. I do hit the wall sometimes and question what I'm doing. I get weary and feel like I'm chasing my tail at times. And then instances like this come up. I get young people all the time who say "You've been an inspiration," "You were the reason I got into theatre," etc. Even some of the kids I'm working with now. It means a lot. And, does inspire me to carry on.

I did know about the guy at Dad's wake, but thank you for the reminder.

I love you!

When you live from the call of your soul, it is like dropping yourself into the pond of consciousness. You have no idea or control over how the ripples unfold and what impact or influence they may have. Even so, the inner feedback of living a life filled with love, peace, joy, connection, and all the experiences you yearn for, including pure bliss, make the effort and the journey the only one really worth taking.

≍

The following concepts summarize living the call of your soul:

- Each soul has a unique calling.

- You have everything you need to accomplish your soul's call.

- The soul unfolds moment by moment.

- When you live your soul's purpose, success is assured.

- Your life purpose is energizing and larger than the tasks you perform.

- Passion is the energizing fuel of the soul.

- Whatever your soul calls you to has a purpose.

- Practice living moment to moment to align with your soul.

- Soulful living reduces stress and improves relationships.

- Soulful living leaves a reverberating legacy.

Practice Living Your Soul's Call

Take one hour with no agenda to move moment to moment with your soul's call.

Write your experience.

Explore stories from your childhood for strengths, talents, and affinities.

Think of three occasions when you felt energized and enthusiastic. What were you doing? What qualities did you bring to the experience?

On what qualities do people compliment you?

Part III
Stepping Into the Call

What you are is what you have been,
what you will be is what you do now.

—Buddha

Knowing the dynamics of the relationship between the ego and the soul, and how you can transform that relationship for a more peaceful, happy, purposeful life is helpful on one level. Yet little actually changes without action.

I read box loads of books and attended many live presentations through my early life, yet still felt alone, lost, and at times in deep despair.

Real change started happening after a few months of therapy with a person who encouraged me to move into the experiential level of awareness. Then I participated in many more experiences, which accelerated the shifts to achieve the life of freedom I enjoy today.

Let your own soul be your guide to the resources that are most useful to you. See what calls you, what attracts you, what resonates with your soul.

Remember: Moving with the soul's call is your unique unfolding process. There is no "there" at which you will arrive in this lifetime, except death. So go consciously and enjoy the scenery along the way. This is a path of self-appreciation in actualization, a path of discovery, and the most challenging and rewarding experience you can ever have.

The supportive resources in this section are divided into three chapters. "Techniques" (Chapter 9) are methods you can learn to use to help in restructuring the ego. "Teachers and Guides" (Chapter 10) are those who can provide expert guidance because, having preceded you on this path, they know the terrain. "Stepping into the Call of Your Soul" (Chapter 11) summarizes key elements in taking action toward living your soul's purpose.

The ego mind restructures through new experiences. Hearing and living the call of your soul is an experiential process. You must take action to get results.

Chapter 9

Techniques

> *To grow, you must be willing to let your present and future be totally unlike your past. Your history is not your destiny.*
>
> —Alan Cohen

Emotional Freedom Techniques (EFT)

> *If you haven't experienced it, it's not true.*
>
> —Kabir

When it comes to remodeling and renovating the original ego structure, there is nothing more effective than the Emotional Freedom Techniques (EFT). Tapping on acupressure points puts a quick and easy way to break free of old patterns of emotion, thought, and behavior at your fingertips. I teach this to all my clients so they can continue to release and create new experiences between sessions. This accelerates the ego restructuring process.

There are two ways to use these techniques: on the surface, to stop a habit or relax your body; and at a core, ego conditioning level, to release ego structures created in childhood.

You can learn the basic EFT technique through demonstration videos online or from a qualified practitioner or teacher. If you put my name in youtube.com or go to my Website (*www.ailaspeaks.com*), you will see my tap-along demonstration video.

Research shows that just tapping the points will reduce cortisol (stress hormone) levels.

Plus, in the hands of a qualified practitioner, you can make amazing progress in transforming the ego structure and releasing core unconscious patterns.

My book-signing table was set up next to Jenny's at a book fair. Her eyes would not stop watering. She said, *"My allergies are really bothering me today!"* I carry antioxidants with me that usually work in minutes for allergic reactions. I offered these to Jenny. Thirty minutes later, there was still no let up in her symptoms.

I asked Jenny if she had ever tried acupressure tapping. *"I've seen it and have not tried it myself"* she said. So, we started to tap on the allergy symptoms and how she felt about having them. Her eyes were not watering quite as much. Then, she noted with surprise, *"The allergies just flared up after I moved here. The only other time was when I moved to Florida. I really loved living there too."*

There is the ego pattern. Jenny learned in childhood there is always a consequence to happiness. Once we tapped on that, her eyes stopped watering. She was fine the rest of the day.

Releasing Grief and Grieving the Loss of the Dream

> *All changes, even the most longed for, have their melancholy; for what we leave behind us is a part of ourselves; we must die to one life before we can enter another.*
>
> —Anatole France

There are two observations I want to share about grief in the transformation process. One is that often we can take on others' patterns of behavior or emotion as a way of remaining close to them once they leave. The other is that, often in order to transform your life to one that is grounded in truth, you may need to grieve the loss of a fantasy or dream.

I had a call from Miriam, who had a lifelong cat phobia. Recently it became worse; she could not leave her house for fear of seeing a cat. We did the EFT technique until she felt calm when thinking about a cat. Then, she called her neighbor to bring her cat over to test our results. She was fine with the cat, and enjoyed holding and petting it. The phobia was gone.

I asked Miriam what happened just before the fear of cats escalated. *"My aunt died five months ago, and my mother passed last month."* As it turns out, Miriam grew up with both of them and *their* fear of cats. She never had a bad experience with a cat. She learned her fear from these women, and when they left, the fear escalated as she tried to stay close to them. We then tapped about her feelings of grief.

Miriam was delighted to be free of her cat phobia and agoraphobia, and felt more at peace with the loss of these two important women in her life. All this was accomplished with about 20 minutes of focused acupressure tapping.

On a personal note, my husband and I had gone through infertility testing and treatments for many years before finally deciding to stop and apply for adoption. After dreaming of being pregnant for so many years, I felt a deep sense of grief. Once I grieved the loss of the dream of pregnancy, I could fully engage in the adoption process with joy and anticipation for parenthood.

What fantasies or dreams are you still holding onto? Losing these can open you fully to the marvelous *real* life your soul has in store for you.

Meditation

> *Calming the mind allows more space for being present.*
>
> —Eckhart Tolle

Meditation is a way to focus the mind. Practicing meditation has benefits for stress reduction and for mental balance, focus, and acuity. It is a method for teaching the mind how to slow down through repetitive focus.

You can focus on anything: your breath, a word or phrase repeated throughout the meditation (mantra), a candle (image). You can also focus on just allowing the thoughts that arise in your mind to drift through like words on a boat floating by. The key is not to stop the thoughts, nor allow your mind to run a whole story or scenario taking your attention away from your focus. When that happens, just come back to your focal point and release the thoughts.

It's important not to judge yourself for whatever happens in your meditation. As soon as you notice that the mind has captured your attention with *You have to go to the store later,* gently bring your attention back to the focal point you have chosen.

Meditation is a practice, not a destination. Having the discipline to sit still for a few moments at a time focusing the mind is enough. Whatever happens during those few moments is fine. Just observe how your mind works and bring your attention back to the focal point.

There are many types of meditation: mindfulness, vipassana (Buddhist), contemplative prayer, transcendental, walking or movement (tai chi, yoga), guided meditation, and more. In guided mediation, someone else's voice leads your mind to focus on certain images that are relaxing or intended to evoke a certain state of being. Explore different styles to find the one that is right for you.

I find that mindfulness and sensing your body are the simplest practices to begin quieting the mind and tuning in to the sensations and intuitions of the soul. You can bring yourself into the present moment by simply sensing your feet on the ground and body in the chair. I start every coaching session with this simple practice.

※

The following concepts summarize ego relieving techniques:

- The Emotional Freedom Techniques (EFT) is a powerful use of acupressure tapping to release conditioned patterns.

- You may adopt behaviors and feelings of others in the grief process.

● It may be necessary to grieve the loss of a dream or fantasy before moving forward in transformation.

● Meditation practice is a useful way to relax and focus your mind.

● Mindfulness and sensing your body is an effective practice for being present.

To Explore a Transformational Technique

Watch the EFT video at *www.ailaspeaks.com/eft.html.*

Think of a stressful situation for you. Assess the stress level on a scale of 0 to 10, with 10 being the worst. Do the tapping sequence all the way through. Think about the exact same scenario again. What is your stress level after the tapping?

Chapter 10

Teachers and Guides

> To confront a person with his own shadow is to show him his own light.
>
> —Carl Jung

Value of a Teacher

> As we look ahead into the next century, leaders will be those who empower others.
>
> —Bill Gates

I feel very fortunate to have many excellent teachers and coaches along with a gifted therapist as guides in my transformation process. I know I would not be where I am today without them. Renovating the original ego structure requires sensitivity, skill, and an emotionally safe environment. These guides were each able to provide those supports.

There are many kinds of guides and myriad approaches. It can be very confusing to know how to choose the right one for you. In the end, your best measure to use is your soul's intuition. There is also information that can help narrow the field of choice. This is the best guidance I can offer from my experience.

First, there are two basic categories of therapeutic modalities: those that work from a primarily cognitive level and others work from a primarily experiential level. If you are addressing general issues in your life, either approach can be helpful. When you are addressing a transformation shift, you need an experiential approach.

Cognitive and behavioral approaches help you to understand the dynamics and issues you face, and support you to make new choices. The limitation of these approaches is that you can still only make choices within the original ego structure of conscious and unconscious beliefs you started with as a child.

Most of my clients are helping professionals who spend many years diligently working on their life issues. They have engaged in a variety of therapeutic approaches and still have a core of fear, sadness, grief, uncertainty, emptiness, loneliness, or other deep unresolved feelings. Or, they experience repetitive behavior patterns that don't seem to change even with all the skills they learn and implement.

For the ego structure to change, you must have radically new experiences that challenge previous beliefs. This is difficult to do alone due to the ego fear that arises as soon as you think about stepping outside the comfort zone of your original structure. That fear, because it comes from the experience of a young child immersed in the emotion of the experience, often feels overwhelming or terrifying.

This is why it is difficult to approach by yourself or resolve from the rational mind. The level of fear is not logical or rational when it happens at the precognitive and preverbal stage of development. To make a change at these early experiential levels, you need experiential approaches.

When parents leave and close the door, a 2-year-old can feel abandoned and like survival is at stake. Mom is still my lifeline at that age. When I am 8 or 9, I might feel uncomfortable and I know I can take care of myself for a while.

Gloria was emotionally estranged from her mother for as long as she could remember. The family had been through many counselors with little success. Even though she was very intelligent and wise at the age of 21, she struggled through high school and now in college.

She took several medications. Gloria had labels of bipolar disorder, attention deficit, depression, and occasional obsessive compulsive behaviors. Her father enrolled in my Emotional Freedom Techniques Level 1 and 2 classes. Because he could bring a guest for the introductory level, he decided to bring Gloria.

Gloria loved the acupressure tapping technique and noticed that it worked to release a school stress issue. She wanted to learn more, so her dad enrolled her in Level 2 for the next two days. In Level 2, people learn how to work on "core issues" from early childhood conditioning. Gloria eagerly volunteered for the first demonstration.

We tapped on her longstanding feeling that her mother didn't love her. That feeling shifted several times through the tapping. Then a memory arose. Gloria saw herself standing behind her 2-year-old self, who was barely tall enough to see out a screen door. She could smell the macaroni and cheese her grandmother was cooking in the kitchen as the little girl watched her mother and father get in a car and drive away.

We tapped on the child's feeling that her mother left her and wasn't coming back. There were many feelings in this moment—sadness, anger, disappointment—she was also happy to be with her grandmother, who was making her favorite food.

When we were done, Gloria said, *"My whole body feels completely different. I feel relaxed and relieved! I see how that moment is the key to everything I've felt about my mother. I felt she went away and left me for good. Now I see she was just going to work."*

Her father affirmed that no matter what her mother did to try to prove to Gloria she loved her, Gloria never felt it was true. Gloria didn't understand why, either. She just knew on a deep level she didn't trust her mother's love. About a month after the class, I received an e-mail from Gloria's father:

> As a result of the session you did with my daughter, she no longer holds any resentment towards her mother. It is like a fresh breeze swept through our home and took all the hate, confusion, distorted thoughts and misunderstanding away. Now a new day is ushered in and my home is filled with laughter and the love of a daughter for her mother. You have given me my daughter back.

New research in neuroscience by Karim Nadar shows that after a memory is recalled, it re-stores differently in the brain. Gloria was able to bring up the experience in a safe environment with an experienced guide, look at it now as an adult, metabolize the emotional elements in it using the tapping technique, and re-store the memory in a new way.

I do not want you to get the impression that transformative experiences always resolve this fast. When a person is young, resolution can be faster because the trauma has not been compounded and reinforced for 40 years. There were also other variables in this situation.

Gloria had a chance to build trust with me the day before this class. Because she and her dad were the only students in Level 2, the environment felt completely safe. Gloria was ready to release this issue and engaged all of her senses in the process. She could even smell her grandmother's macaroni and cheese cooking. Other factors include my expertise with the transformation process and EFT, the level of presence held by both me and her dad, and entrainment.

What to Expect From a Teacher

Teachers open the door...
You enter by yourself.

—Chinese proverb

There are some qualities and conditions you can expect from any qualified counselor, therapist, coach, or guide. These are non-judgment, a safe environment to share your deepest thoughts and feelings, confidentiality, knowledge and skill to help you explore what is important to you and your soul's unfolding, and support for your ongoing ability to make choices and sustain your progress after your time with them is complete.

Helpers are like alpine guides in a chalet at the base of the Alps, ready to assist the next person who wants to climb the mountain. They are all equipped with certain maps and tools.

Some have only trekked the lower slopes. Others climbed a single peak to the top. They are experts in that specialized terrain. And, still others are Sherpas, who have climbed nearly all the highest peaks, know the pitfalls and risks, and can take you anywhere you want to go safely.

If you have general concerns or dissatisfaction in your life, most credentialed guides can help you. If you have a specific issue, you may want a specialist who has depth of experience and success in that area. Specialties are issues such as addiction, PTSD, marriage counseling, and others.

When you are ready for a major life change or transformation, you want someone who continuously engages in his or her own personal growth and knows the deep terrain well. You want a Sherpa.

These are general guidelines. You don't need to overthink your choice or let yourself be stuck with the idea of making the wrong choice. If you have explored a few possible options, trust your heart on which guide feels right to you. After all, it was a psychic with no counseling credentials who knew how to guide me in handling the night terrors.

Roles of the Teacher or Guide

When fears are shared in a space of loving kindness, with the intention to release them, they diminish and even disappear.

—Layne and Paul Cutright

The teacher or guide can help in a variety of ways. Here are a few.

As a Guide to the Next Level

In the ancient mystery schools, they always advised having a guide or guru (teacher), as it was thought you could go crazy if you were not in the hands of a teacher who knew the pitfalls and the way through this territory.

We do not know what we have not experienced. Moving into new territory requires new knowledge and skills. Your guide can teach you what you need to know and support you in taking the necessary steps to proceed safely.

You don't need to be married to be a good marital therapist or have children to be a skilled family therapist. To be a transformation guide, however, you must have personal experience with the transformation process. The big difference is that transformation is experiential and can be terrifying at moments. You need someone who can maintain the confidence, centeredness, and presence that come from living through transformation.

Not all guides engage in their own ongoing inner growth. In terms of transformation, you want someone who is working on his or her own inner life all the time. You want a person who has an orientation toward growth as a continuous process rather than a final destination.

As a Clear Mirror to See Your True Self

Parents are the first mirrors for how we see our self. Those mirrors are composed of beliefs and ego structures that distort the image they reflect. When you go through transformation, you want a clear mirror that will not distort your view with its beliefs or judgments.

This is essential in all transformative processes. In the therapy process, the 12-step process, or the spiritual transformation process, it is important for the person with whom you are working to be an unbiased, non-judgmental witness to your revelations.

Being in the presence of a witness who observes and accepts you as you are is a profound healing experience. The fifth step in the 12-step process involves sharing your self-inventory with another human being. A parallel example in the spiritual process is the practice of confession.

Sharing with another human being who you are and what you have done, and being heard and accepted, "warts and all," is transformative in itself. This experience opens the door to releasing the past and seeing yourself in a clear authentic way.

Entrainment—Presence

Your guide is a model for what is possible, for where you want to evolve. Just being in the presence of someone with a lighter vibration of energy or consciousness can influence you. *The teacher has been where you are going, so being in his or her presence helps you entrain to that level of vibration.*

HeartMath scientists have shown that heart-brain interactions can occur from one individual to another. Your heart can communicate with another person's brain.

A 1999 HeartMath study, *The Role of Physiological Coherence in the Detection and Measurement of Cardiac Energy Exchange Between People,* found that "When two people are at a conversational distance, the electromagnetic signal generated by one person's heart can influence the other person's brain rhythms."

How to Know When it Is Time to Move On

'Come to the edge,' he said.
They said, 'We are afraid.'
'Come to the edge,' he said. They came.
He pushed them—and they flew.

—Guillaume Apollinaire

You may start on the lower slopes of the mountain with a guide who helps you explore and acquire the basic skills to live comfortably with growth and change. This may be all you need for a while. When you feel confident to sustain the new knowledge and skills on your own, you might want to fly solo.

You might want to move from the lower terrain up a specialty peak. It will be time to find a specialist to help you get to a new level. You can outgrow a teacher or hit the boundary of his or her capacity. When you are engaged in the transformation process, though, you want to evaluate the desire to quit too soon.

When you are a person who has an inner drive to learn all you can about yourself and unfold your soul to its fullest, then you are exploring with a Sherpa. There will be times when you want to quit. Your ego mind will create reasons or excuses to stop prematurely, especially when a big shift is right around the corner.

Be sure to discuss any thoughts about ending the relationship with your guide directly. He or she can help you to determine if you are ready to stop because your growth is complete to that point, or if you are about to breakthrough to a new place and your ego wants to avoid that shift.

Just know that finding new guides as you grow and change is fine. It does not indicate that your original or current helper is deficient in any way. Each of us has different skills and talents, and each client has different needs as time goes on.

At the same time, be aware that sometimes your urge to change guides may be a sign that inner change is imminent. Don't leave in haste. Discuss your decision with your guide first.

Investment

Be patient with yourself. Self-growth is tender;
it's holy ground. There's no greater investment.
—Stephen Covey

In difficult economic times or when limited finances are part of your issues, it may be hard to justify spending money on engaging a coach, counselor, or other guide. When your soul calls you to this process, you can generally find a way. Living the soul's journey involves taking the first step and being open to how the goal may be met in unexpected ways.

When I was wondering how I could pay for the program I needed, notices started arriving in the mail for 0-percent credit cards. At that time, the percentage rate when 0 percent ran out was only 6 percent. I financed my transformational programs on 0-percent credit cards. I'm *not* recommending this approach to you. I would not use this method today. I don't know what might show up for you.

Weigh the cost against the potential benefits. The investment in time and money for appropriate guidance may save you many years of struggle, pain, and stuck-ness. It may also bring you to new heights of success and prosperity in all areas of your life efficiently and effectively by releasing unconscious blocks.

Look upon your counselor or coach's fees as an investment in yourself and your life success. Coaches and counselors can shortcut your learning curve by years, thus opening you to greater success. Use your own intuition.

My vision for you is that you attract the perfect guides to help you expand the boundaries of belief in your potential and possibilities toward living the call of your soul.

⚹

The following concepts summarize the value of a teacher or guide in the transformation process:

- For a transformation shift, you need an experiential approach.

- Transformation is difficult to do alone due to the ego fear that arises.

- Qualities of an effective guide include non-judgment, safe environment, confidentiality, knowledge, and skill to explore conditioning and sustain ongoing progress.

- Transformational guides continuously engage in their own personal growth.

- Use your intuition and the call of your soul to determine the best guide for you.

- Your ego mind may create reasons to quit just before a breakthrough.

- Always talk with your guide before discontinuing with them.

- See your guide's fees as an investment in yourself.

To Explore Available Teachers or Guides in Your Area

Play the role of a researcher or investigative reporter who is writing a report on transformational change and looking for a person to interview. Talk to at least three different types of guides.

Chapter 11

Stepping Into Your Call

Things do not change; we change.
—Henry David Thoreau

Decision

*The most difficult thing is the decision to act;
the rest is merely tenacity. The fears are paper
tigers. You can do anything you decide to do.
You can act to change and control your life,
and the procedure—the process—is its own
reward.*

—Amelia Earhart

Once a decision is made, everything becomes easier; it almost becomes inevitable. I have noticed this in
myself and my clients. Ralph Waldo Emerson captured it:
*"Once you make a decision, the universe conspires to make
it happen."*

Edie and I devoted several sessions to the dilemma of
staying in a job she hated or taking the risk to leave and

start her own business. One day, as she was walking out the door, she said, *"I'm done. I don't know what's going to happen. I just know I'm done."* Then, she turned to me, exclaiming, *"I feel better already!"*

The next week, Edie couldn't wait to tell me what happened. *"The day I handed in my resignation I got a call from a customer who wants to commission me for several projects!"* It wasn't easy getting to the decision to change, yet once the decision was made, everything started to fall into place effortlessly.

This is the way the soul works. It prompts and prods your ego, raising the discomfort level until you finally decide to make the change that releases whatever is standing in the way of unfolding your next soul call. Then, and only then, do the doors of opportunity open wide for resources to appear.

When will you make your decision to step into the call of your soul?

Action

> *It had long since come to my attention that people of accomplishment rarely sat back and let things happen to them. They went out and happened to things.*
>
> —Leonardo da Vinci

Reading this book provides a map for a new way to live a life filled with the experiences you most desire. A map is just a map. It shows you the way, yet it cannot take you where you want to go. You must take actions that move you toward your destination.

There are so many options. You can go to the end of each chapter and choose a suggestion that speaks to you. You can call that counselor, coach, or guide you have been thinking about seeing to set an appointment. If you have been numbing your pain with some substance or other destructive habit, you can take an action to stop or locate a treatment center or 12-step group right now to start removing that barrier.

Christina Grof talks about addiction as a part of a "spiritual emergence" process. Recovery reconnects you with your soul. Recovering people frequently say they are grateful for the addiction, because it brought them to a way to reclaim their self. The rest of the population thinks living in the Well is "as good as life gets."

The ego structure will not change without a radically new experience. Taking a deliberate and conscious action toward living the call of your soul is a powerful way to claim your intention. Whether the action is helpful or not is not as important as doing it. Action communicates intention—hence the truism "actions speak louder than words."

What action can you commit to your soul to take before you close this book?

Trust

> *When you come to the edge of all the light you know,*
> *And are about to step off into the darkness of the unknown,*
> *Faith is knowing one of two things will happen:*
> *There will be something solid to stand on*
> *Or you will be taught to fly.*
>
> —Barbara J. Winter

The biggest barrier to taking action for a change is the ego's fear of what might happen. Rather than trying to suppress or argue against the ego, take a look at what the ego is trying to protect you from. Acknowledge the risk, and weigh the costs and benefits on both sides of the equation.

When I considered taking the action to divorce, my mind went around and around, trying to decide what to do. I knew in my heart and soul I had to do it, yet the uncertainty of the outcome caused my mind to be stuck. I asked myself, *"What is the worst that could happen?"* The answer finally came down to *I could end up in a homeless shelter.*

What would happen then? I wondered. At that point, my mind started listing the skills and talents I had to rebuild my life. I saw myself helping the other women, friends offering job opportunities, a new place to live. I started to feel lighter, hopeful, energized. It was amazing!

The ego is clueless about the future so it doggedly clings to the present: *"Don't change anything! We don't know what will happen."* When you engage in the dialogue between the soul and the ego, the soul invariably wins. The ego knows the past; the soul knows the possibilities!

You have already lived through your past. There is nothing there that will throw you for a loop. Also, I've never seen nature grow backward. It always opens into new growth and diverse possibilities. Your soul is the seed for your unfolding life. When you open to the soul's call you open to your divine inheritance.

Can you trust enough to make a decision, take an action, and see what happens?

※

The following concepts summarize stepping into your soul's call:

- Once a decision is made, opportunities appear to step into your soul's call.

- Nothing changes until you take an action.

- The future is unknown to the ego mind.

- Taking action requires trust in the unfolding purpose of the soul.

To Explore a Stepping Into Your Soul's Call

Assess your level of discomfort with the status quo of your life now.

Do you feel your soul is calling you to grow in a new way?

Make a decision to explore the call.

Commit to taking a specific action to let go of a barrier to stepping into the call.

Write down what happens!

Index

chakras, 161

change, elements of,
107-108

childhood, 21, 28, 31, 35,
43, 61, 63, 75, 100, 101,
117, 126, 127, 169, 171,
191, 217, 222, 223

children, 35, 43, 52, 66, 67,
174, 207, 236

choice, conscious, 25, 52,
62, 63, 87, 90, 119

Chopra, Deepak, 168, 173

clarity, 37, 46, 47, 49, 170

co-dependence, 102, 128

communication, 161

conditioning, 53, 61, 63,
84, 92, 132-134, 162, 163,
174, 177, 192, 213, 222,
232, 242

conformity, 66, 101, 133

consciousness, 25, 59, 74,
147, 162, 165, 169, 214, 238

control, 21, 211, 212, 214
feeling in, 178-180
illusion of, 68

conviction, 47, 66, 157

creative questions, 175

crisis, 126, 129-132, 153,
154, 191

cultural expectations, 15, 172

curiosity, 23, 25, 35, 37, 66,
74, 85, 97, 105, 143, 154,
191, 201

despair, 102, 126, 127-129,
153, 219

Diamond Heart Approach
(ital?), 23, 37, 60, 109,
139, 148

diet, 81, 123

dieting, 134, 197

disorientation, 126, 138-
141, 154, 158

distraction, 102, 122,
127, 208

About the Author

AILA ACCAD, RN, MSN, is an award-winning international speaker, best-selling author, and certified life coach, who began her quest for the purpose of her life at age 9. She became an energy healer, Reiki Master, and stress expert in the process of exploring numerous wisdom paths. As president and founder of LifeQuest International, LLC, she shares uniquely simple experiences to help clients hear and live their call of the soul. Thousands have achieved self-knowledge and stress freedom through her groundbreaking process, *Breaking the Perfection Myth,* and best-selling book, *34 Instant Stress-Busters.* As stress expert and healthcare futurist, she is a popular keynote speaker and radio and television guest. Aila lives in an A-frame home in the beautiful hills of Charleston, West Virginia, where she hosts classes and retreats.